I0155809

Living Gracefully

Practical Proverbs for Women: Book 2

Living Gracefully

Practical Proverbs for Women: Book 2

Dara Halydier

Scripture taken from the New American Standard Bible, The Lockman Foundation, California

ALL RIGHTS RESERVED

No part of this publication may be reproduced, stored in a retrieval system, or transmitted, in any form or by any means—electronic, mechanical, photocopying, recording, or otherwise—without prior written permission from the author.

© 2018 Dara Halydier
All rights reserved.
ISBN 10: 0-9851239-8-2
ISBN 13: 978-0-9851239-8-7

Endorsements

"Rarely have I come across a resource as helpful as Practical Proverbs for Women. Dara Halydier clearly communicates timeless, godly principles in a pragmatic manner. She is an able guide and her teachings should inspire transformative changes!" – Dr. Les Carter, Christian psychologist and author of *The Anger Trap*.

"We all have difficulties from time to time with depression, anxiety, fear or loneliness, and Jesus has the answers. Dara helps her readers find the solutions in Scripture. Living with chronic pain has given Dara the opportunity to walk hand in hand with Jesus seeking His wisdom, strength, and power to her thru each day. *Living Beautifully* and *Living Gracefully* give her readers the opportunity to learn from Dara what Jesus has taught her, so we can walk hand in hand with Jesus, too. – Ellen K. Moore, Med, LPC (Licensed Christian Counselor)

"I just want you to know how mightily God used you in my life when you taught at my church. I am a perfectionist and Satan was running away with my emotions. Thank you for being honest with your struggles and sharing the answer through God's word. I literally cling to those Scriptures. His Work is life!!! Thank you again." – D.S.

"I'm pretty picky about Bible curriculum. So much of what I find is way too fluffy or worldly and isn't worth using. There are a few gems I found, though, and Practical Proverbs by Dara Halydier is one of those." – The Old Schoolhouse Magazine

Other books by Dara Halydier:

Living Beautifully: Practical Proverbs for Women Book 1
Practical Proverbs for Younger Students (Ages 8-15)
Practical Proverbs for Older Students (Ages 15-young adult–homeschoolers can get high school credit.)
Wisdom, Work, and Wealth (12-week Bible study for 5th grade through adult)
As They Sit and Stand: A Resource and Guide for Teaching Your Child the Bible

You can see these books at *www.abidingtruthministry.com*

Dedication

I dedicate this book to several friends that have sharpened me like iron sharpens iron (Prov. 27:17). Thank you Deja, Ellen, Hope, Kathy, Leigh, and Sherri. You make my life bright and beautiful! I am blessed to call you my friends.

I also dedicate this book to five amazing sons who continue to teach me every day about living life to its fullest. They bless their parents regularly. Thank you, Garrett, Nathan, Aaron, Ethan, and Lucas.

Practical Proverbs for Women: Living Gracefully Book 2

Butterflies are deep and powerful representations of life. Many cultures associate the butterfly with our souls. The Christian religion sees the butterfly as a symbol of resurrection and new life for those who believe in Jesus Christ. Around the world, people view the butterfly as representing endurance, change, hope, and life. May your study through Living Gracefully help you to fly above your circumstances and give you strength to endure and persevere to see your hope realized in eternity with God.

Practical Proverbs is a two book Bible study course for adults with an emphasis on life management skills. *Living Beautifully: Practical Proverbs for Women Book 1* (8 weeks) covers Proverbs 1-9 systematically, and *Living Gracefully: Practical Proverbs for Women Book 2* (8 weeks) covers Proverbs 10-31 topically. They can be done as a group or independently.

Living Gracefully will look at the book of Proverbs by pulling all the verses on a topic together and then applying the whole counsel of God's word to that subject. Topics include: pride, humility, money management, contentment, diligence, our words, anger management, honoring your body, honoring your parents, marriage, child-rearing, and the Proverbs 31 woman. Being able to file away God's wisdom, proverb by proverb, will lead you into a victorious and rich life in Christ Jesus.

Each student will do five lessons per week individually and then get together for a teacher to go over discussion questions once a week. There are suggestions for the teacher at the end of each five lesson week.

Unless otherwise mentioned, the Bible verses are taken from the New American Standard Bible.

God's Word is eternal and thus, foundational for every person. May God bless the study of His Word and bring you long life and wisdom and joy.

Introduction

The fear of the Lord is the beginning of wisdom (Proverbs 9:10), but once we have gained some wisdom and understanding, we need to apply it to our lives. What does holy living look like? Is it possible to live a pure and holy life in the 21st century?

It *is* possible to live holy and pure before the Lord in the world today. Proverbs has some great precepts that will help you navigate through some tough circumstances that life may throw at you. The Proverbs are backed up by the rest of Scripture and are fulfilled in Jesus Christ.

You are about to embark on the laying aside of your old nature and putting on your new nature with a practical study through Proverbs concerning various topics concerning you as a Christian living in a secular world. The writer of Proverbs is good King Solomon. Even though he wasn't perfect, he learned from his mistakes and sought God's wisdom. You can also.

Corinthians 2:16 says that as a believer, you have the mind of Christ. If wisdom is the ability to judge correctly and use our knowledge to avoid trouble, solve problems, reach goals, and succeed in life based upon God's principles, then having the mind of Christ is the key.

Romans 12:2 says, "Do not be conformed to this world, but be transformed by the renewing of your mind." A renewed mind is the mind of Christ, and you acquire the mind of Christ by reading His Word, talking to Jesus, and asking Him for wisdom.

Colossians 3:2 reiterates this principle. Write this verse here: _____

_____

_____

As you study *Living Gracefully,* my prayer for you is that you will find joy in following the Lord's commandments and find freedom in seeking out His kingdom and His righteousness.

Practical Proverbs for Women: Living Gracefully

History of Pride

*Pride goes before destruction
and a haughty spirit before stumbling.*

Proverbs 16:18

I was an achiever. My self-esteem was wrapped up in how I performed. In high school, I was the first chair French horn player and the first-string pitcher on the softball team. I was a straight A student, a person with good morals, a leader in my church youth group and involved in ministry. My flesh looked pretty good. I was depending on myself rather than God who gave me any talent or ability I had.

I went to college and crashed. I was working three jobs, taking 19 hours of course work, working out with the softball team, playing in the band, and had roommates who were drinking, smoking pot, and involved in other immoral activities. I began living out of my car. My family had moved away and offered no support or advice. I cratered and found myself in a situation I couldn't get out of and decided not to resist. I was raped. Then I spiraled and started drinking. I tore my shoulder and could no longer play softball.

I hit bottom, and there I found God waiting for me. I humbled myself before Him, and He has replaced my need to perform with His grace and unconditional love. My flesh was just as icky as the drug addict's, the prostitute's, or the murderer's. Mine was just wrapped up in a fancier package. It took all of God's blood to save me and all of His grace to restore me. But, oh the joy that comes from understanding who I am in Christ and who my God is.

Peace and joy came in when I put my pride in my accomplishments aside and realized that only in Christ am I a worthy treasure. Pride is putting yourself before God. Pride is thinking you are in charge and taking the credit for something you could not have done without the Lord. Pride was Satan's sin that got him kicked out of heaven. Pride was Eve's and Adam's sin that got them kicked out of the garden. Born again Christians are saved by grace and won't get kicked out of God's family because of sin (see Romans 8:1), but they can be excused from God's presence. Your fellowship with God can be broken due to thinking more of yourself than you should. Pride can seep into your worship, your dreams and goals, your memories, your actions, your words, and your relationships. Pride is a heart-sin.

Look up Mark 7:21-23. Listed among this infamous group of sins is pride.
Where do these verses say pride comes from? _____

Outward sins are usually the first ones that we point a finger at, but just as insidious and deadly are sins of the heart. Actually, outward sins are almost always the demonstration of heart-sins. James 1:14-15 says that temptation leads to lust, lust to sin, and sin leads to death. This is the LSD principle: lust (your thought life), sin (your actions), death (the consequences). Don't think sin for a Christian won't lead to death. You have eternal life with Jesus Christ, but this earthly life is still in peril as well as others' lives. May it never be that your sin would lead another to his/her or your own death.

In 2009, World Magazine reported that a public figure had committed adultery. He was a Christian, and his fall began when he thought he didn't need accountability. He had several Christian men warn him to stay accountable to an individual or a group as he headed into public service, but he thought, "That won't ever happen to me. I can handle this." [My paraphrase]. As he was tempted and his support group was not there to confront him, his lusts gave way to sin and most assuredly led to the death of a marriage, death of trust, death of his job, death of respect. His pride had cost him.[1]

Let's look closely at this sin of pride and see some examples, God's thoughts on pride, the results of pride, the opposite character trait of pride, and God's command about pride over the next couple of days.

Satan's Downfall:
Read Isaiah 14:12-15.

Isaiah is prophesying here about Babylon and how Israel will glory in its fall. Prophecy, however, often has double meanings, and many commentators believe these verses also describe Satan's fall from heaven. Babylon is often associated with the world system which is Satan's realm.

Satan was the head archangel. His job was music leader. He was to lead the angels into worship of the Holy, Heavenly, Creator God.

According to Isaiah 14:11 what led to Satan's downfall? _____
_____

Pomp is another word for arrogance.

In verse 13 you can see the intent of his heart. "But you said in _____ _____, 'I will ascend to heaven; I will raise my throne above the stars of God, and I will sit on the mount of assembly in the recesses of the north. I will ascend above the heights of the clouds; I will make myself like the Most High'"

Satan began to think he was important and began to demand that others bow down and worship him. He thought he was equal to or greater than God Almighty. The result of his pride is shown in verse 15: "Nevertheless, you will be thrust down to Sheol, to the recesses of the pit." (Sheol is an ancient word for hell or the eternal abyss.) This prophecy has not yet been fulfilled.
Revelation 12:4, 7-9 is also a depiction of Satan's fall from heaven to earth and how he took one third of the angels with him. These we call demons. Satan is reigning here on earth until the end of times (1 John 5:19)

when according to Revelation 20:1-3, he will be overthrown and bound and cast into the abyss for a time. Eventually, Satan will be thrown into a lake of fire for eternity (Rev. 20: 10), but he is not through yet. He desires to convince humans as well to follow after him rather than God.

Adam and Eve's Downfall:

Look at the first sin of mankind in the perfect garden and perfect relationship with God. Satan decided if he couldn't rule in heaven, he would rule here on earth. After all, he wanted to be like God. In Genesis the first couple were walking with God. All of their needs were met. They lived in a lush garden with all the green plants for food. They walked with God, up-front and personal. They were welcomed into His presence. Enter Satan, seen here as the serpent. He lies to Eve and claims if she eats of the forbidden fruit of the Tree of the Knowledge of Good and Evil she will not die as God has said, but rather she will be like God. Sound familiar? Enter pride.

Eve lusts to be like God and takes the fatal bite. The consequence of her sin is indeed death, and death was brought to all mankind by her choice. Don't get prideful and think you would have handled circumstances differently! Each of us has made choices based upon the same heart-sin–pride.

Your Downfall:

There are examples all throughout the Bible and history of men and women making fatal mistakes based upon pride–wanting to have more power and prestige than is their due. Nebuchadnezzar is one example. God humbled him with a mental illness (Daniel 4:24-37). David is another example. He thought he could stay home from battle and just be king. His pride led him to adultery and murder (2 Sam. 11:1-5,14-15).

Hitler, Stalin, Mussolini, and the other statesmen of the WWII era all fell to pride and took millions of lives. The Roman Empire fell under the pride of the Caesars.

What has your pride cost you? _____
Has your pride kept you from making a commitment to Jesus Christ? _____
Has your pride brought heartache to others and severed their trust? _____
Has your pride destroyed opportunities to serve God? _____

I remember a time when I knew God was prompting me to tell a young couple about Him. My pride kept me from telling them the good news. I have many times since prayed that God used a more faithful follower to reach them. But what if they didn't hear the Word and die in their ignorance. My pride may have kept them out of heaven.

Each of us deals with pride. But this sin can be overcome to a great degree. It is a battle you must take on minute by minute, day by day. When you stand in the presence of your eternal, holy, almighty God, all pride will vanish. Until then, you will study ways to defeat it.

Questions to think about:

How can you overcome pride?

1. Are you willing to give it a try?

You might have memorized Proverbs 3:1-12 in *Living Beautifully: Practical Proverbs Book 1*. For the next 8 weeks, you will continue memorizing this chapter. Turn to appendix A and draw pictures or highlight words to help you memorize Proverbs 3:13-14. If you have Proverbs 3:1-12 memorized, you might want to review it every day.

God's Thoughts About Pride

The fear of the Lord is to hate evil;
pride and arrogance and the evil way
and the perverted mouth I hate.

Proverbs 8:13

According to Proverbs 8:13, what are God's thoughts about pride? _____

Look at what God says about pride, arrogance, boasting, haughtiness, and trusting in yourself.
James 4:16 says, "But as it is, you boast in your arrogance; all such boasting is _____."

Look up Proverbs 6:16-19. God hates six things and seven things are an abomination to Him. What is the first
on the list? _____ That's pride!

Proverbs 21:4 says: "Haughty eyes and a proud heart, the lamp of the wicked, is _____."

Does God take pride seriously? The Scriptures say He hates pride. Why do you think this is? _____
_____
_____
_____

God created man in His own image. He knows how special you are, and He loves you. He created you to need
Him and to have a vital relationship with Him. When you are trusting in your own methods, talents, goodness,
etc., then you are denying your rightful place in God's creation. He has created you a little lower than the
angels, but not above Himself.

2 Corinthians 3:5 reminds you, "Not that we are adequate in _____ to consider anything as coming
from ourselves, but our adequacy is from _____."

He is your breath, your life, your very being. You are to work with Him but never forget that without Him you can do nothing (John 15:5). This applies to all men. Look at John 1:3. "All things came into being through Him (Jesus), and apart from Him _____ came into being that has come into being. In Him was life."

Look also at a couple of other verses which put your existence into perspective.

1 Corinthians 8:6: "For us there is but one God, the Father from whom are _____ things and we exist _____ Him; and one Lord Jesus Christ, by whom are _____ things, and we exist _____ Him."

Colossians 1:16 -17: "For by Him _____ things were created, both in the heavens and on earth, visible and invisible, whether thrones or dominions or rulers or authorities— _____ things have been _____ _____ Him and _____ Him. He is before all things, and in Him _____ things hold together."

So instead of being prideful, you should be worshipping and thanking God for your very existence! As a born again Christian, how much more you should recognize pride as sinful. You did not save yourself. You did not die for mankind. You cannot earn your way to heaven. It is only by God's grace and mercy that you can have an intimate relationship with your very Creator. When you realize this and accept that all that you are and all that you have is from God's hand, then there is no room for pride.

Let's define pride. Pride is an exaggerated self-esteem—thinking more of yourself than what is true. You are God's child, His prince or princess, but, you are not God. You are not in charge. You are not on the throne. God is! Self-esteem should not be based on how pretty you are, what other people think about you, or on how well you perform at any given task. Its basis should only be the fact that God made you and you are His. You may not always act like a princess, or feel like a princess, but the truth remains if you are a child of God's, the King of Kings, you are a princess.

It is good to like yourself (Galatians 5:14: "Love your neighbor as yourself."). It is good to feel approval for a job well done. It is even good to go to bed knowing you lived the best you could that day, but always keep in mind that you are because God created you. You have a relationship with Him because He died for you. You are able because He has given you specific talents, gifts, and purposes. Let thanksgiving be always on your tongue.

To finish up today's lesson, look at Proverbs 25:27. What are God's thoughts about pride?
"It is not good to eat much honey, nor is it glory to search out one's own _____."
You are probably wondering what eating honey has to do with pride, right? Honey is good for you. But too much honey can give you a bad stomachache. Feeling good about yourself is also good for you, but seeking your own glory will make you sick spiritually.

Proverbs 27:2 says, "Let another praise you, and _____ your own mouth; A stranger, and _____ your own lips."

Seek to do God's will, to know Him, to be obedient to His commands, and He will lift up whom He lifts up, and He will put down those whom He puts down. There is a lot of relief in this reality. I don't have to promote myself; I can trust God to open doors and shut doors and bring me to the mind of others in His time. I can concentrate on just being the best me in Christ I can be. God will take care of the rest. This goes against the world's principles, but remember you are not of this world. You are of a better, more everlasting world! You belong to the King of Kings!

Because God hates pride, He has placed a judgment on it. Read Proverbs 16:5. "Everyone who is proud in heart is an abomination to the Lord; assuredly, he will not be _____."

God further declares in Isaiah 13:11, "I will also put an end to the _____ of the proud and abase the _____ of the ruthless."

Proverbs 29:1 describes a man who in his pride, *hardens his neck* or becomes stubborn and prideful. Suddenly, the prideful man will be broken beyond remedy, for there is no remedy for pride. If man is not willing to repent and step down from the throne of his own life and let Christ rule in all areas, then there is no salvation, no remedy.

Questions to think about:

1. What is your self-esteem based upon (looks, performance, or others opinions)?

2. What should your self-esteem be based upon?

3. How does this help you to avoid pride?

4. Start memorizing Proverbs 3:13-14.

> How blessed is the man who finds _____
> And the man who gains _____.
> For her profit is better than the profit of _____,
> And her gain is better than fine _____.

Week 1 / Day 3

Being Humble

A man's pride will bring him low,
But a humble spirit will obtain honor.

Proverbs 29:23

So if you are not to be proud, how should you position your heart? What is humility? What does humility look like? How do you live it out? Let's look to God's Word for the answers.

Read Romans 12:16. "Be of the _____ mind toward one another; do not be _____ in mind, but associate with the _____. Do not be _____ in your own estimation."

Let's break this verse down. First, humility is being of the same mind as other believers. This means not putting yourself above them in your own mind. A Christian should not look at other Christians in judgment, but rather in love. If a younger Christian doesn't have the knowledge or discernment you have, you are not better, just farther along on the journey God is taking you on. God may have a different journey for your Christian brother or sister. Your attitude, in this case, should be one of gratitude towards God. He has taught you and trained you so you can discern and teach others. Humility is being grateful.

When I was in my 20's, I tended to be very judgmental. There was a right way and a wrong way. As I have gotten older, I have come to understand that on many topics, there are no right and wrong, just different options and opinions. (There are some non-negotiables such as morality and basic tenets of Christianity). I have to choose what God has called me to do; I do not have to judge others because God may have called them to do something different (dress, education, raising kids, how I worship, etc.).

Do you tend to be judgmental of someone who does things differently from you? _____
If your answer is yes, ask God to soften your spirit and begin seeking ways of offering grace to those who are different from you.

The next part of the verse talks about not being haughty in mind but associating with the lowly. Your thoughts should not be prideful. This will lead to your actions not being haughty, but rather you will desire to reach out to those less fortunate or who are not in the same place in their life journey as you are. You should be grateful, act gratefully, speak gratefully, and demonstrate your gratefulness through service to others.

Finally, the verse ends with a good reminder, "Don't be wise in your own estimation." It is possible to act humbly without being humble. But this is falsehood and will eventually reveal itself. If you squeeze a sponge with water in it, water will come out. If circumstances squeeze a person who has pride, pride will come out. It may show itself in anger, self-pity, or arrogance. If a person of humility is squeezed, he/she will remain humble, forgiving, and kind.

When was the last time you were squeezed by life's circumstances? _____
_____
_____

What was your response?
    a.) hurt and anger
    b.) self-pity
    c.) arrogance
    d.) humility and concern for others

There are a lot of promises from God's Word for the humble. Look these verses up and write down the rewards of humility.

Proverbs 22:4 _____

Proverbs 21:29 _____

Proverbs 18:12 and Proverbs 15:33 _____
_____

Your answers should have included riches, honor, life, a sure way (confidence), and more honor.
So, you can see God would desire you to be humble and there is great reward in humility, but how do you grow in humility?

You saw from yesterday's lesson that the first attitude you must adopt is proper positioning before the King of Kings. He is on the throne, you are not. Today you learned the second secret to humility—gratitude. You need to be thankful for all God has given you and done for you and thankful for the people in your life, your circumstances, and for whom God made you to be. There are physical attributes or circumstances in each of our lives we wish God would change. Being grateful for them instead of resenting them is a big step towards a humble attitude. Just accepting that God knows what He is doing in your life and that all situations, good and bad, comes through His hands, can lead you to having a grateful heart.

Proverbs 30:11-14 describes an arrogant, prideful man. "There is a kind of man who _____ curses his father and does not _____ his mother." A humble person then would thank his father and bless his mother in word and in action. These verses also say, "There is a kind who is pure in his own eyes, yet is not washed from his filthiness." A humble person is quick to acknowledge when they are wrong and quick to repent to God for sin.

Continuing on you read, "There is a kind–oh, how lofty are his eyes! And his eyelids are raised in arrogance." A humble person is content where God has placed him and satisfied with the fruits of his labors, not looking to others wishing to be something he is not.

And finally, "There is a kind of man whose teeth are like swords and his jaw teeth like knives to devour the afflicted from the earth and the needy from among men." A humble man is not stepping on others to get what he wants, but rather he reaches down and helps those who are less fortunate or are younger.

Let's list some characteristics of a humble person.
1. Has a good understanding of his relationship with God
2. Is grateful
3. Blesses his mother and father and others in word and action
4. Acknowledges when he sins and is quick to repent
5. Is content and satisfied with his lot in life
6. Is giving and compassionate towards others

A quick note about number 3. Some people have parents who are easy to bless and others have parents who are not respectable. If you are in the latter category, know that God will honor your efforts to be respectful even if you only get grief in return. You will cover this more in detail in a later chapter on parents.

How do you compare with the six characteristics of a humble person? _____
_____
_____

Take some time in prayer to ask God to reveal to you any area that you are still prideful about and ask Him to make you humble. Beware, God answers your prayers!

Questions to think about:

1. How do you compare to each of the definitions of humility?

2. Overall, would you say you have an attitude of pride or humility? In what areas do you need to work on becoming more humble?

3. Practice memorizing Proverbs 3:13-14.

   How _____ is the man who finds _____
   And the man who gains _____.

For her _____ is better than the profit of _____,
And her _____ is better than fine _____.

Pride vs. Humility

He who trusts in his own heart is a fool;
But he who walks wisely will be delivered.

Proverbs 28:26

Today you will see the reputation pride brings and some commands from the Lord about pride. But first, let's review. What is the opposite of pride? _____

List 6 characteristics of a humble man from the last lesson.

1.
2.
3.
4.
5.
6.

Here are some verses to look up.

Proverbs 11:2 "When pride comes, then comes _____, but with the humble is wisdom."

Proverbs 14:16 "A wise man is cautious and turns away from evil, but a fool is _____ and _____."

Proverbs 21: 24 "'Proud,' 'haughty,' 'scoffer,' are his names, who acts with _____ pride."

List some of the characteristics of a prideful man according to these verses.

1.

2.

3.

4.

5.

6.

7.

A biblical fool does not recognize God and lives his life in reckless abandon until the final judgment. A prideful man goes one step further and does not recognize who God is, but places himself on his throne as God. For him there is no hope. Our hope is in Jesus Christ alone, and the only way to Jesus is through the humbling of your spirit to recognize your own inadequacies and the need of a Savior. Pride is the wall that stands in the way for many a man to come to Christ.

As a Christian, pride is a wall that can keep you from a deeper walk, a more intimate fellowship with your Lord and King. Pride comes from the prideful one, Satan.

There is a fine balance between loving yourself as a creature of a wonderful Creator and worshipping yourself as better than you really are. Fighting pride is a lifetime battle. Pride can ruin a marriage, break the hearts of your children, leave you without friends, lead you into homosexuality and other perversions, and keep you from the presence of God. Be quick to recognize your sins or mistakes and be quick to repent and apologize. Keep current on your confessions.

In marriage and in parenting, I find that if we all have a servant's heart as we encourage one another, then pride doesn't get in our way (too much)! The ability to give grace to others comes when you have fully received and understood God's grace, and you realize you could never pay the debt for sin. God graciously freed you from the power of sin. In comparison, others' debts against you are not that great. If God can forgive others, then who are you to hold something against another? When you realize to what extent God has poured His grace out upon you, you will be filled up and overflowing with grace for others. Someone who has not experienced God's grace, cannot extend grace to others. Are you a grace giver? _____

Lastly, there are some verses that are a command and will set you on your way to stand before the King (Prov. 22:29) and as an ambassador to the Mighty King (2 Cor. 5:20).

Proverbs 27:2 "Let another _____ you and not your own mouth, a stranger and not your own lips."

Proverbs 25:6-7 "Do not claim honor in the presence of the king, and do not stand in the place of great men; For it is better that it be said to you, ' _____ _____ _____,' than for you to be placed lower in the presence of the prince whom your eyes have seen."

As you work on this study of Proverbs and look at other areas of your life, keep in mind pride is often at the root of all other choices. Ask God to dig up any pride in your life and make your heart humble before Him.

Questions to think about:

1. If you boast, what should you boast in? (Jeremiah 9:23-24)

2. In what areas of life are you tempted to boast about yourself?

3. Practice memorizing Proverbs 3:13-14.

How _____ is the _____ who finds _____,
And the man who _____ _____.
For her _____ is _____ than the _____ of _____,
And her _____ is better than fine _____.

Humility Through Obedience

The mind of man plans his way,
But the Lord directs his steps.

Proverbs 16:9

So that your faith would not rest on the wisdom of men,
But on the power of God.

1 Corinthians 2:5

Pride can be your downfall. Humility can be your victory! Having a true understanding of who God is through the study of His Word and of who you are in comparison is quite humbling. But you are not to have a low self-esteem. Your self-esteem should be based on your position in Christ. You are a fellow heir and princess of the King of Kings! Your response to this should not be one of pride, but one of gratitude and thankfulness.

Is your self-esteem reliant upon performance, other's opinions, or the way you look? _____
_____

What should your self-esteem be based upon? _____

And now that you know your position, you can bend your knees to the Lord and understand what Isaiah 55:8-9 means.

For My _____ are not your _____,
Nor are your _____ My _____," declares the Lord.
"For as the heavens are higher than the earth,
So are My ways _____ than your ways
And My thoughts than your thoughts.

Humility is acted out in trusting God and being obedient to His Word, His ways, and His voice. This should be a relief. When you act in obedience to God, the results are His responsibility not yours. Obedience requires listening, and listening requires a relationship and conversation with God.

Write John 10:27. _____

_____

_____

Are you hearing God's voice today? Years ago I was praying about hearing God's voice, and I found Peter Lord's book called, *Hearing God.* His book begins with this poem by Louis Eberly.

> Love must express and communicate itself.
> That's its nature.
> When people love one another, they start telling
> Everything that's happened to them.
> Every detail of their daily life, they "Reveal" themselves
> To each other, unbosom themselves
> And exchange confidences.
> God hasn't ceased being Revelation any more
> Than He's ceased being Love.
> He enjoys expressing Himself.
> Since He's Love. He must give Himself,
> Share his secrets, communicate with us
> And reveal Himself to anyone
> Who wants to Listen.[2]

So the first key to hearing God is to want to listen. Reading and studying the Scripture is a good way to know about God, but you grieve the Holy spirit when you ignore the Author and don't get to know Him personally.

Peter Lord says, "The great tragedy is that most of us only come to God in crises. We move from crisis to crisis and never learn that we need him and his words for every part of life. Until hearing God becomes vital to you and me, we are not likely to learn to hear either quickly or correctly."[3] When something is vital to us, it literally means that we will die without it.

How vital is hearing God to you? _____

To hear God, you must line up your value system and priorities with His Word. You must make hearing God your number one priority. This requires perseverance and practice. There are times I think that I hear God, but am not sure. I do know that God never goes contrary to what He has said in the Bible. I have decided that if I think I hear God speaking, I am going to act on it. Period.

Last week, I felt impressed upon by the Holy Spirit to include three of our earlier edition books of *Practical Proverbs* for teens in my crates as I packed for a convention. The last hour of the last day, a woman came to my booth. She needed three of the Older Student books of *Practical Proverbs* and two younger student books. She could not afford all of them. God reminded me of the three earlier editions which were in my crate. I was able to bless her with a lower price, and she will be able to do this study with all of her children.

I remember attending a Christmas pageant one year put on by a local church. It was held in a large community theater. The rows of chairs were close together and each chair was very near its neighbor. My family sat down and then had to stand again to let a young couple through. They had multiple piercings, lots of tattoos, and chains. I was intimidated by them. She sat right at my elbow in the seat next to me. I prayed for them throughout the program and thought I heard God tell me to say something to them. I struggled with this for the whole program and rose and left with my family without having uttered one word to them. I felt immediately that I had let God down. My disobedience may have kept them from heaven. Now, I know God forgives, and His grace will cover my sin, but I grieve the lost opportunity.

Since that pageant, I have made my goal to be to follow through on whatever God wants me to do no matter how uncomfortable I feel about it.

Can you recall a time in your life you heard God and didn't listen to Him? _____
_____
_____

What about a time you heard God call and you did listen? _____
_____
_____

In John 15:11 Jesus says, "These things [His commandments] I have spoken to you so that My joy may be in you, and that _____ joy may be made full." As you listen and obey God's voice, you will find joy!

Once you hear God, you must act upon His words. This is trust and obedience. What about the outcome? Pretend you are going to fry an egg and you don't want to break the yolk. There is a difference if a task was your idea or God's idea. Fill out the chart below with the words *success* or *failure*.

Objective	Whose assignment	Yolk broke	Yolk is whole
Don't break yolk	mine	_____	_____
Don't break yolk	God's	_____	_____

Your answers should have been failure and success for the first line and success and success for the second line. In your wisdom, you failed if the yolk broke and were successful if it remained unbroken. But in God's wisdom because He asked you to do it, you are a success no matter what the outcome is because you obeyed!

This is true no matter what it is you are doing in obedience to God. If God has asked you to speak and witness to others, even if no one accepts Jesus as their Savior, you are a success if you go and witness. If God asks you to minister to your neighbor, but all she does is grumble at you, you are still a success!

God wants your obedience, and the results are His to direct. There is freedom in this. If you listen to God and obey, you will always be successful in His eyes. In this is wisdom.

Questions to think about:

1. What are some ways you hear God's voice?

2. Do you spend time during prayer to listen?

3. Are you quick to obey?

4. Say Proverbs 3:13-14.

Week 1 Group Discussion

For a thorough discussion of these questions refer to the Leader's Guide in the back of this book.

1. In what areas or relationships do you battle pride? (Mark 7:20-23, 1 John 2:16)

2. How can you overcome this pride? (Matthew 23:12, Matthew 18:23-35)

3. What should your self-esteem be based upon? (Eph. 2:4-10, Col. 1:13-23, 2:10, John 1:12)

4. What is your self-esteem based upon?

5. How does a proper understanding of who God is and who you are in Christ help you to avoid pride?

6. In what areas of life are you tempted to boast about yourself? (Psalm 34:2, Proverbs 27:1-2, Proverbs 25:14, Jeremiah 9:23-24, 2 Corinthians 12:9, Hebrews 3:6, James 3:5)

7. What are some ways you hear God's voice?

8. Do you spend time during prayer to listen?

9. Are you quick to obey? (John 15:10, Acts 5:29, 5:32, Romans 6:16, 2 Corinthians 10:5, Hebrews 5:9, 1 Peter 1:22–ordering your thought life to be obedient to Christ Jesus).

10. Quote Proverbs 3:13-14 together.

Trusting in Riches

Two things I asked of You,
Keep deception and lies far from me
Give me neither poverty nor riches;
Feed me with the food that is my portion,
That I may not be full and deny You and say,
'Who is the Lord?'
Or that I not be in want and steal,
And profane the name of my God.

Proverbs 30:7-10

Money. It's necessary. Is it evil? How much is enough? What should our attitude be about money? Is a poor man more spiritual than a rich man? Is being rich wrong?

Proverbs answers all of these questions, but a broader view at the Bible will also help you to clarify your answers. Over the next several lessons, you will be looking at God's Word and His attitude towards money.

As always, God looks at your heart. Are your motives pure? Do you want money for selfish gain? Is money a reflection of your worth? Or is money a means to accomplish God's purposes in your life?

Several verses in Proverbs give you some clues about how you should look at money. Look at Proverbs 30:7-10 above. What two things did the writer of Proverbs ask God for?

1.
2.

Notice the balance. He doesn't ask for riches, but he does ask not to be poor. Let's examine some attitudes often related to having much money and attitudes related to not having enough money.

In the above verses, what was the temptation of the rich? _____

What was the temptation of the poor? _____

The rich man realized he was self-efficient and didn't need God, whereas the poor man stole in order to live and by doing so went against the law of God. When you break the law of God, you are, in essence, saying you don't trust God enough to provide; you take the bull by the horns and depend upon yourself. Isn't this the same thing the rich is guilty of doing? Either extreme leads to denying God, God's power, God's provision, God's goodness, and God's love.

Proverbs 23:4-5 says, "Do not weary yourself to gain wealth, cease from your consideration of it. When you set your eyes on it, it is gone, for wealth certainly makes itself wings like an eagle that flies toward the heavens."

Matthew 6:33 gives you Jesus' perspective on what you should consider. According to this verse what should you seek? _____

What is the word *all* referring to in this verse? _____

If you are not sure, go back a few verses and read verses 24-25. That's right! God promises you that if you focus on the kingdom of God, He will provide your needs–food and clothing! Are you going to trust Him?

Riches are fleeting. Ask someone who gained their wealth in the stocks and bonds of the 1920's. During the great crash of the 1930's, many went from top floor executives to basement bums. Many committed suicide. And again, in 2008, many lost homes and resources due to the home mortgage bubble busting.

Use the following chart and compare these verses.

	Those Who Trust in Riches	The Righteous
Prov. 11:28	will fall	will flourish
Prov. 15:16	_____	fear of the Lord
Prov. 28:6	crooked	_____
Prov. 16:8	_____	righteousness
Prov. 11:4	no profit	_____
Prov. 10:16	_____	_____
Prov. 28:20	punishment	_____

You might have memorized Proverbs 3:1-12 in *Living Beautifully*. Verses 5-6 say to "Trust in the _____ with all your heart and lean not unto your own understanding, in all your ways acknowledge _____ and He will make your paths straight." This includes your finances. We, as Americans, are so richly blessed that we forget to give God the glory and to depend on Him, but He is God of our finances as well as our souls.

We lived in a parsonage in an inner-city community when we got a phone call from the EPA (Environmental Protection Agency). "Get out of your house, go somewhere immediately and wash all of your clothes." Black toxic mold had been discovered at toxic levels in our home. We grabbed our sleeping children and got them settled in the car. We drove around for about an hour in shock until we were finally able to call another pastor who allowed us to come crash at their house. We borrowed clothes to wear while ours were washing.

With the insurance company dragging their feet and the church divided about whether black mold was really toxic or not, we ended up homeless for about two weeks. Eventually we were able to move into a furnished apartment until all of the details could be worked out. We didn't know if anything was salvageable or not. About a week into the ordeal my emotions were running rampant and I needed to get by myself and cry and pray. I left my family and our friends in tears and headed to the car. Once the engine started, the radio automatically sounded. "God is in control," the music gently reminded me. I went from crying to laughing. So what if we lost everything we owned, God is bigger and will supply all my needs according to His riches in Christ Jesus! (Phil. 4:19).

I went back into the house laughing and praising. I'm sure everyone thought I had lost my mind! We were eventually able to retrieve most of our belongings after they had been washed thoroughly with biocide (death to all life). God provided through friends during that time and my release of possessions brought contentment and joy in the midst.

Questions to think about:

1. How important is money to you?

2. Do you put your trust in riches or God?

3. Have you ever had an experience of needing something you just couldn't afford, and God provided for you?

4. Are you rich and don't need God or poor and always worrying about where your next dollar will come from?

5. How can you begin to have a proper attitude about money?

6. You will be adding Proverbs 3:15-16 to your memory verses this week. Turn to Appendix A and under line or highlight key words. You might also draw pictures or make up actions.

How Much Is Enough?

It is a blessing of the Lord that makes rich,
And He adds no sorrow to it.

Proverbs 10:22

How much money do you need to have enough? What amount will make you content? What must your salary be for you to be happy? These are all common questions, and you may have a ready answer. Unfortunately, people across every economic level have found that *enough* is always *a little bit more*, so they continue to pursue the dollars and never have *enough*.

Contentment is the key to financial success. Now, in everything there is the need for balance. Being content out of laziness is not going to bring happiness either. You will study work ethic and God ordained work in a couple of days. But today, let's focus on contentment.

Paul says in Philippians 4:11-12 that he has learned to be content in what circumstances? _____
_____

Wow! The only way this is possible is through the grace of God and through praise to Him in everything. Go back a few verses to Philippians 4:6. This is the key.

> Be anxious for nothing, but in _____ by prayer and
> supplication with _____ let your requests be made
> known to God. And the peace of God, which surpasses all comprehension,
> will guard your hearts and your minds in Christ Jesus.

Contentment, then, is being at peace with God about every circumstance, trusting Him to take care of your needs.

You learned yesterday that you should first seek God's _____. In Philippians 4:19 you read, "And my God will supply all your _____ according to His riches in glory in Christ Jesus."

Sometimes trusting God means redefining what is a need and what is a want. If you are truly walking in righteousness, having been born again through Jesus Christ, are truly seeking His kingdom, are walking in obedience in an intimate relationship with Him, and giving thanks to God in every situation, then He will meet all of your needs. What a promise! What relief!

An important concept to learn is that you are to trust God. Period. You are not to trust that He will give you possessions, or do something for you, or change your circumstances. You are just to trust God. He knows all things and loves you and wants the best for you. You ask, but you may be asking amiss because you do not see the whole picture. If your faith is in God and not in what He will do for you, then when you are caught in the storms of life and circumstances don't turn out the way you want them to, you can still trust that God is in control and has a purpose and plan for all things pertaining to your life.

Fear is the opposite of trust. If you have fear of the future, of how God is going to meet your needs, of not having enough, etc., then you are not trusting God. What do you fear? _____
_____

While John the Baptist was baptizing in the desert preparing the way for Jesus, Messiah, several groups of people asked him what to do to prepare for the coming wrath. His response is found in Luke 3:11-14. He told those who had two tunics to share with those who had none, and for those with food to share with those who had none. He goes on to tell the tax collectors to be honest in their dealings and not to collect more than they are supposed to. To the soldiers he said not to take money from anyone by force and not to accuse anyone falsely. He also told them in verse 14 to, "Be _____ with your wages."

Hebrews 13:5 says, "Make sure that your character is free from the love of money, being _____ with what you have; for He Himself has said, 'I will never leave you, nor will I ever forsake you.'"

Wealth is fleeting. If you put your trust in money, your trust will be broken. But, "Jesus Christ is the same yesterday, today, and forever" (Hebrews 13:8). Put your trust in Him and you will be forever taken care of. Jesus never promised you wealth, rather He promised tribulation (John 16:33). Here is a *Treatise on Suffering* I wrote when I was struggling with some hard circumstances.

> Why does God allow suffering in our lives? This has been answered a hundred times over in books, articles, sermons, etc. But, I believe I have stumbled upon one of the best explanations that will take God off the hook, allow Him to be worshipped as sovereign and good, and brings hope to the heart of the sufferer. It all has to do with perspective.

> If we believe in a God who promises us a life of ease and comfort, health and wealth, then we are not following the God of the Bible. No, Jesus is realistic when He says that to follow Him we must take up our cross and follow Him. He says that in this life we will face persecution and troubles, heartaches and heartbreaks. He says do not be overcome by these troubles because we are not of this world. That's right. It's about perspective of where we live.

> When Adam and Eve sinned in the garden, Satan was given dominion and authority over mankind and

this world. He is the prince of the air, the lord of the earth. The earth was given to every kind of illness, debauchery, decay, and heartbreak man has ever known. We live in a garbage dump ruled over by the great deceiver. Living in a garbage dump will bring stink and decay. One cannot be in a garbage pit and not get garbage on them. The stench is in the very air we breathe! One of Satan's greatest deceptions is that as Christians we should be above our earthly dwelling and should experience only good and right and blessings.

We go about expecting to live on cloud nine and become frustrated and unbelieving when we see the reality of our garbage dump. We coast along expecting good things to encounter our path and when something goes astray so does our faith. In reality we should expect nothing but garbage. We live in a garbage pit! Then when troubles come, we know where they came from, why they came, and how to endure through them.

When good things happen, what a miracle! What a joy! What a reason for rejoicing! In times of illness or defeat, we look to our Savior who will one day remove us from the garbage pit and set us on cloud nine. But for now He promises His wisdom to avoid some of the garbage from splashing on us, and His presence and His comfort when they do. And that is enough. In great pain, great loss, great confusion born of this world there is hope. Hope for the future (heaven) and hope for the minute by minute dealing with the trouble (His presence and comfort).

When you lose your job, get sick, lose a loved one, face a giant, or are slandered or afraid, remember when you live in a garbage pit, it stinks! But God sent His Son to give us a way out and a way through. He is faithful and kind. Look to Him. We are not of this world (1 John 2:15-17, 4:5-6, 5:18-19).

How does this perspective differ from the traditional Christian perspective? _____

_____

_____

Learning to be content in the midst of the garbage dump takes supernatural power—power that comes only from a close walk with your Savior.

Questions to think about:

1. What heart condition should you learn in regards to money?

2. Do you expect things to go well and blame God when they go wrong or do you expect things to go wrong and praise God when they go right?

3. Who is the god of this world? Who wins in the end?

4. Are you content in whatever circumstance life finds you in?

5. Work on memorizing Proverbs 3:12-15.

How blessed …
And the …
For her …
And her …
She is more precious than _____;
And _____ you desire compares with her.
Long life is in her _____ hand;

In her _____ hand are riches and honor.

Greed

Four things are small on the earth,
but they are exceedingly wise:
The ants are not a strong people,
But they prepare their food in the summer;
The shephanim are not mighty people,
Yet they make their houses in the rocks;
The locusts have no king,
Yet all of them go out in ranks,
The lizard you may grasp with the hands,
Yet it is in kings' palaces.

Proverbs 30: 24-28

When you think of majestic, proud animals does the ant, the shephanim (a small rodent like a chipmunk), the locust, or the lizard come to mind? No. When you think of majesty and power, what animal do you think of? _____. I think of a lion. And yet, God uses four of the smallest creatures to teach us a lesson about pride and provision.

When you think about powerful people, who comes to mind? _____

You may have written Donald Trump, Barak Obama, Oprah, Bill Gates. These are people who have riches and power on the national scene, but are these godly, wise people you should emulate? _____

God provides for the small creatures by giving them the instincts to survive. The ants know to store food for later, the shephanim know to build their houses in the rocks for protection, the locusts know to stay together for food, and the lizard is able to live in the palace of the king! If God loves you more than these, then He will provide your needs as well. And He provides in grand style!

When our family first moved to Fort Worth, Texas, to attend seminary, my husband was out of a job for about 8 months. We had three children at the time who needed to eat. God provided a part-time job for me at a preschool two days a week which met some of the basic needs of our family and still allowed me to homeschool kindergarten with our oldest. We still had a house in North Dakota we were making payments on as well. We had a garage sale one month and made $1 more than the house payment! When we were down to our last can of soup, someone put some groceries on our front porch and another time there was money in the mailbox. To this day I do not know the donors of these generous gifts. Christmas time came and there was no money for presents. We got a call to go and look in our car. Someone had put a few gifts for the boys in the front seat! Easter came and I needed hose. My secret pal from the preschool included a pair in a basket of Easter goodies. Throughout this entire time, we had not made our needs known to man; we simply prayed and waited upon the Lord. He is faithful and true! In recent years God has provided buyers for a house, college scholarships for five sons, and money for music lessons, and we have never missed a meal.

Wealth and pride often go hand in hand. Let me state here that God has given wealth to a few people that it might be used for his kingdom, but generally it is a little bit given graciously by many that makes up the vast amount of contributions to churches and ministries. "And to those to whom much is given, much is required!" (Luke 12:48)

Here are a few Proverbs reiterating this point.

28:11 "The rich man is wise in his _____ _____, But the poor who has _____ sees through him."

18:11 "A rich man's wealth is his strong city, and like a high wall in his own _____."

10:15 "The rich man's wealth is his _____, The ruin of the poor is their poverty." (Remember your lesson on extremes. This is poverty born out of laziness.)

If a rich man puts his trust in his money and makes this his stronghold, his security, then it is a false security. This false security will lead to greed. He might think, "If I need money to be okay, then more money will make me more okay." Proverbs 11:6 tells you what becomes of a greedy man. "The righteousness of the upright will deliver them, but the treacherous will be caught by their own greed." Greed is the opposite of contentment. Contentment is found in a grateful heart.

Take a minute and list the things you are grateful for.

1.	6.	11.
2.	7.	12.
3.	8.	13.
4.	9.	14.
5.	10.	15.

Do you trust the Lord to provide for your needs? Proverbs 10:3 reads, "The Lord will not allow the righteous to hunger."

Read what Proverbs 13:25 has to add; "The righteous has enough to satisfy his _____, but the stomach of the wicked is in need."

That should assure you that God will provide for your needs of food and sustenance. For your need of shelter and a place to dwell, Proverbs 10:30 says, "The righteous will _____ be shaken, but the wicked will not dwell in the land." Proverbs 14:11 gives us confidence that: "The house of the wicked will be destroyed, but the tent of the upright will _____." God is equipped to, "Meet all of our needs according to His riches in glory in Christ Jesus," (Philippians 4:19).

This verse not only includes your material and financial needs, but also your emotional needs. Once I was feeling unloved and unlovable. My parents had disowned me, my in-laws had walked out on us, and my husband was very focused on his career. We had just moved to a new town. A lady from church invited me to go shopping with her. As she tried on clothes, I browsed a rack of dresses. One dress in particular, stood out to me. It was my colors and very pretty. I didn't mention this dress to her or anyone else.

About a week later, I was visiting with a homeschool mom and I told her my story and that I was feeling very lonely and depressed. A few days later she called and said she had told my story to her mother and her mother wanted to bring a gift by for me. She showed up to my house with the dress that I had noticed at the store! Right then, I knew God loved me, and that I was lovable because He died for me and cared for me. To this day, whenever I wear that dress, I feel the arms of Jesus wrap around me. He knew my need and met it unexpectantly!

We joke at our house when we have a financial need that God owns the cattle on a thousand hills (Psalm 50:10), and I hope He will slaughter and sell one for us!

Questions to think about:

1. What are your basic needs?

2. Has God provided for your needs?

3. Tell of a time when God unexpectedly provided more than your needs financially or emotionally.

4. Work on your memory verses.

   How blessed …
   And the …
   For her …
   And her …
   She is more _____ than _____;
   And _____ you _____ compares with her.
   Long _____ is in her _____ hand;
   In her _____ hand are _____ and honor.

Giving

He who gives to the poor will never want,
But he who shuts his eyes will have many curses.

Proverbs 28:27

Today you are going to look at God's economy. It is much different than the *take care of number one* philosophy of this world. Look at the following verses and fill in the chart.

	The World's Way	**God's Way**
Life:	Cling to it	Matthew 16:24-25
		_____
Material needs:	Get all you can	Matthew 6:33
		_____
Enemies:	Get revenge	Matthew 5:44
		_____
Money :	Get it, horde it	Matthew 6:19 Luke 6:38
		_____
Relationships:	Independence	Matthew 18:3
		_____

As you can see, God's economy is not the same as the world's system. There are several references in the New Testament to giving away money or possessions in order to gain material needs or eternal life. Giving away your possessions will not gain you eternal life unless it is an outward sign of an inward change of repentance and faith. But many so cling to their material wealth for security, they must release it in order to gain a relationship with Christ. This is another premise of God's economy: sometimes you must let go of something in order to gain something better.

Read the story of the rich man who asked Jesus what he must do to get into heaven in Mark 10:17-27. What might be something one must let go of in order to gain a right relationship with God? Here are a few examples to get you started: sins, dreams, time. Now you add a few more. _____
_____
_____
_____

I had a group of women do this at a retreat and we came up with about 50 different things one might be asked to yield, or give up to God to gain a right relationship with Him. Others included singleness, job aspirations, desire for a family, health, and addictions. These are things you must relinquish the right to have or to be in control over, knowing God has a plan for each of us and that plan may include or not include some of the things you have set your eyes on.

Does that make God a killjoy? Should you expect a life with no pleasures or desires? No, there are just different pleasures and desires you can have. The greatest being the pleasure of spending time with a God who loves you deeply. Maybe God didn't give a woman the ability to have children, but instead she was able to adopt and nurture several orphans or abused children to maturity. God always has a plan for what you might consider your failures or shortcomings.

My friend is believing her "momentary, light affliction" (2 Cor. 4:17) of cancer will lead her mom to eternal glory. She is willing to bend to God's allowing the cancer and is choosing to live in belief and joy in the midst knowing salvation for her mom is eternal while her pain is but temporary. Living a victorious life in Christ Jesus is about keeping an eternal perspective.

Let's focus in on money. It is necessary. But you should learn to be content with what God has allowed for you in the context of the work He has provided for you. Money should not be gained falsely, and what you have you should share cheerfully with others. Here are a few more Proverbs about giving to the poor.

Proverbs 29:7: "The righteous is concerned for the rights of the poor, the wicked does not _____ such concern."

Proverbs 22:9: "He who is generous will be blessed, for he gives some of his _____ to the poor."

Proverbs 21:13: "He who shuts his ear to the cry of the poor, will also cry himself and not be
_____."

Proverbs 19:17: "One who is gracious to a poor man lends to the _____, And He will repay him for his good deed."

Proverbs 18:23: "The poor man utters supplications, but the rich man answers _____." This means that as the poor man asks for help the rich man turns him away.

Proverbs 17:5: "He who mocks the poor taunts his _____; He who rejoices at calamity will not go unpunished."

Proverbs 14:31: "He who oppresses the poor taunts his Maker, but he who is _____ to the needy honors Him."

Proverbs 11:25: "The generous man will be prosperous, and he who waters will himself be _____."

Jesus gives a word about this in Matthew 25 in the illustration of the sheep and the goats. Read this story in Matthew 25:31-46. Again, eternal life is not gained by righteous acts, but rather those who know Jesus and have been changed by Him will desire to do good deeds for others and thus is an outward manifestation of an inward change. As a Christian, you are to be about taking care of those less fortunate whether they are there by their own hand or by their circumstances, or by the sins of others.

Let's get practical. You see a man on a street corner begging for money. You don't know his story. Your first reaction is that he probably brings in more money every year than you do. And there are panhandlers out there who make a good living. You don't know what to do.

What does God say? Give, but use discernment. I might give him a sandwich or a bag of groceries. I will not give him money he can use on alcohol. If he insists he needs money for a doctor's bill, I can offer to go to that doctor's office and pay the bill. We give to organizations that have a good track record of helping the poor. We avoid offers to help those that can't give an account of the how the funds are actually used.

My husband has been in the ministry for many years. He will sometimes offer someone a job if they are really in need. It may be painting a wall or digging a ditch. If they are really in need they won't mind working for a couple of hours. Then the church has an agreement with a local gas station and grocery store. We give the needy person a voucher and they can get gas and food, but not cigarettes or alcohol. We are to give, but we should give responsibly. And don't forget to tithe to the Lord from your income (10% or more).

Questions to think about:

1. What are you holding onto that God is asking you to release to Him?

2. Can you trust God enough to let go and trust Him to meet all your needs in His way?

3. How might you give to the poor?

4. Are you responsible for what someone does with that which you give them?

5. Are you tithing?

6. If your response is, "No," which church or ministry will you begin to send your tithe?

7. Work on your memory verses.

How …
And the …
For her …
And her …
She is more _____ than _____;
And _____ you _____ _____ with her.
Long _____ is in her _____ _____;
In her _____ hand are _____ and _____.

False Balances, Surety, and Borrowing

A false balance is an abomination to the Lord,
But a just weight is His delight.

Proverbs 11:1

There are three business practices mentioned several times in the book of Proverbs. These are false balances, surety (usury), and borrowing. You will look at all three of these today.

False balances:

In the ancient world, bartering was used for purchasing goods. One might have bartered a round of cheese for a vessel of wine. Weight measures were put into use to make sure of a fair trade. Later, gold and silver became the means for exchange, and again they were measured by weight. Scales were two trays on a fulcrum. A certain item's price was determined by its weight. If a dishonest merchant balanced the scale so the buyer owed more than was truly fair that was called false balances.

This dishonesty goes against the very nature and character of God. "Jesus is the Way, the Truth, and the Life" (John 14:6). Truth is the very essence of God. False balances go against the truth and is, thus, "an abomination to the Lord."

Read Proverbs 16:11. Why are scales and balances of concern to God? _____

_____

God is concerned with every area of your life. If you are "a new creature" (2 Corinthians 5:17) in Christ, then you were remade from the inside out when you asked Jesus to be your Lord. You don't get to pick and choose the areas of life you want Him to control. He wants to be in control of everything because He loves you and knows as long as you hold on to any areas, you are not fully devoted to Him and are trying to serve two masters—yourself and God (Matt. 6:24). This is why your business practices are of concern to your Heavenly Father.

Read Proverbs 20:10 and Proverbs 20:23. These verses reiterate God's hatred of falsehood.

Surety/usury:
"He who increases his wealth by interest and usury
Gathers it for him who is gracious to the poor."
(Proverbs 28:8)

Surety is loaning money at interest. In the early days of the nation of Israel, loans were not for capital (money needed to start a business), but rather for daily necessities. The Hebrews were admonished in Deuteronomy 15:7-10 to lend to the poor. Read these verses and fill in the blanks.

> If there is a poor man with you, one of your brothers, in any of the
> towns in the land which the Lord your God is giving you, you shall not
> _____ your heart from your poor brother; but you
> shall _____ open your hand to him and shall _____
> lend him sufficient for his need in whatever he lacks … You shall
> generously give to him, and your heart shall not be grieved when you
> give to him, because for this thing the Lord Your God will bless you in
> all your work and in all your undertakings.

God is concerned not with the gift but the attitude and character of the giver. If you lend for the sake of earning money, it is not a pure motive. You should lend that others might benefit. You should give out of love and compassion not out of selfish gain or ambition. Stewardship is a term many Christians use when describing their relationship to their money. Money is not something you possess but rather a tool that has been given to you by God to be used for His kingdom. You are a steward or overseer of your money. It is your responsibility to use it wisely. When you realize money is not yours in the first place—it belongs to God, then you don't mind giving it back to God for His purposes.

Now, if you know any history of the Jewish people to the present day, you know they are known for moneylending. Does this not go against the command of God? Yes, it does. But the Jewish people first rationalized this occupation because they did not loan money to other Jews, only to foreigners. Both Jeremiah and Ezekiel condemned the practice of surety (Jer. 15:10; Ex. 18:13). But unfortunately this practice continued to thrive. After the exile, Nehemiah took "vigorous measures to terminate the abuse."[4] (Neh. 5:1-13)

The Romans' Twelve Tablets laid out harsh punishment for those unable to pay a debt. By the time of Jesus, a regular bank had been set up in Israel. None of this, however, repeals God's commandment. His commandments are always based upon His character, and His character does not change. Loaning money out at interest for basic needs is wrong even today.

Borrowing:
"The rich rules over the poor,
And the borrower becomes the lender's slave."
(Proverbs 22:7)

Surety is strongly prohibited in Scripture, but borrowing, although not forbidden, is warned against. Either you trust God will be your Provider, or you take that role into your own hands. When you are in charge and aware of the world's system of credit, it is easy to justify borrowing money. You may think you can control the circumstances around paying the debt back. Unfortunately, you can't see the future, and events may come up keeping you from being able to repay a debt—a loss of a job, an economic slump in the national economy, other bills, etc. Even though Scripture does not forbid you to borrow, it does give you fair warning that if you borrow you become a slave to the lender until you can pay back the amount due.

Proverbs 22:26-27 warns, "Do not be among those who give pledges, among those who become guarantors for debts. If you have nothing with which to pay, why should he take your _____ from under you?"

Many good Christian organizations give advice against borrowing, but they also realize that in today's economy buying a house would be impossible without a loan. There are smart ways to borrow for a mortgage. Larry Burkett suggests you save up for a large down payment, buy small, pay it off, then sell the house and use the equity to purchase a bigger house which you should still be able to pay off quickly.

College loans are another issue in today's world. Whether you are in college or have a child in college, there are ways to get through school without incurring a great debt load. The first is hard work. My oldest son worked two 40 hours a week jobs during summer months and a part time job during the school year. Between work and scholarships, he was able to get through his first four years with only a very small debt which he paid off the next year by working at the college teaching debate and taking Master level classes for free. He finished that degree as well. He worked for the law group which represented his university for two years of his law degree for free.

Secondly, look for scholarships. They can come from unexpected sources. My third son wanted to get a degree in agriculture. He spoke to the agriculture teachers and found out being a member of the livestock judging team comes with a good scholarship. Never having judged before, he learned a lot and got paid to do it! Thirdly, look at cheaper options such as junior colleges and online courses. Dual or concurrent enrollment is free or very inexpensive in some states and can save you up to a year's tuition.

Hard work is usually the first answer to this difficult problem of borrowing. The second and equal answer is contentment. How much do you really need that new car, that bigger house, those fashionable shoes, etc.? Be wise and prudent. Be patient and save up for purchases. This will bring you much less hardship in the long run, and you will see the hand of God work if you choose to wait upon His provision instead of trying to obtain things on your own.

Questions to think about:

1. What is the heart issue behind false balances?

2. Give an example you have come across about false measurements.

3. What is the heart issue in usury?

4. What is the heart issue in borrowing?

5. Give an example of how borrowing turned out to be a bad idea in your life.

6. Recite Proverbs 3:13-15 out loud.

> How …
> And the …
> For her …
> And her …
> She is …
> And nothing …

How to Set Up a Budget

Commit your works to the Lord
And your plans will be established.

Proverbs 16:3

This verse assumes you have a plan. A budget is a monetary plan. It is naïve to believe that if you make money and spend it without a plan, everything will work out. Proverbs 14:15 puts it this way: "The naïve believes everything, but a sensible man _____ his steps."

There are a lot of good Christian books on setting up a budget. The main thing is not the format but that you have a budget and you stick to it. Budgeting is simply an exercise in writing down how much money you make and how you will spend it. To get started, write down any regular amounts you receive such as a wage earned from a job, a regular birthday gift, or other income. Keep track for a couple of weeks on how you spend your money. Be reasonable. If you spend $40 on gas a week, don't budget $30. What you have on paper won't work unless it matches what you do in real life.

List below your income and expenditures. You can do this by month or year. If you write out a monthly budget, be sure to include putting some aside for Christmas and birthday gifts and other once a year expenses.
Income:

> Job
> Gifts
> Other

Expenditures:

> Tithe
> Savings
> Gas
> Food
> Car payment and maintenance
> Entertainment

Clothes

Gifts

Toiletries

Medical expenses

Medical insurance

Life insurance

Electricity/gas

Water/sewage

Debts

Groceries (include your paper goods and cleansers)

Home maintenance

Taxes

Other

Miscellaneous (unexpected things like postage, haircuts, etc.)

Mad money (a few dollars for which you don't have to give account)

The total income should equal the total expenditures.

When I first started using a budget it was easier for me to actually have envelopes with headings on them for each category. I would then place the amount of money allotted to each category in the correct envelope. When I ran out of money in that envelope, I either didn't spend any more on those items until the next payday, or I shared from another envelope and paid it back the next payday. This was very effective. Sometimes I would run short in the same envelope month after month, and I knew I needed to change my budget.

Now we are sophisticated and have a computer program that sets up our envelopes. But the concept is the same. This program even spits out monthly and yearly reports so we can manage our money wisely. We use Crown Money Map Financial Software. They even have an internet based program called Mvelopes[5] which attaches to your various bank and credit card accounts. We find this a very effective way to see the big picture and be able to deal with the details.

Even with budgeting software, you need to keep on top of your budget. We spend about an hour a week in-putting all of our receipts and balancing our checkbook. Payday usually requires a couple of hours to pay bills. Budget your time as well as your money and realize the investment will bring great dividends in time.

Luke 16:11 is a good reminder for you about how you should use your money. "Therefore if you have _____ _____ _____ in the use of wealth, who will entrust the true riches to you?"

I have a friend who decided to stay home with her kids and save more money by couponing than by going to work. She has done just that! Her pantry is stocked, her kids are at home with Mom, and the bills are paid!

Week 2 Group Discussion

1. How important is money to you? Do you put your trust in riches or God? (1 Tim.6:10, Matt. 6:24)

2. How can you begin to have a proper attitude about money? (Eccl. 5:10, 1 Tim. 6:10, Phil. 4:11)

3. What heart conditions should you learn in regards to money? (Phil. 4:11, 1 Thess. 5:18)

4. Do you expect things to go well and blame God when they go wrong or do you expect things to go wrong and praise God when they go right? (Romans 8:28)

5. Who is the god of this world? Who wins in the end? (Eph. 2:2, 2 Cor. 4:4, John 12:31, Romans 16:20, Rev. 20:1-3, 10)

6. Tell of a time when God unexpectedly provided more than your needs financially or emotionally.

7. What are you holding onto that God is asking you to release to Him? (Mark 12:14, Romans 6:13, 1 Cor. 6:12)

8. Are you responsible for what someone does with what you gave them?

9. What is the heart issue behind false balances?

10. What is the heart issue in usury?

11. What is the heart issue in borrowing?

12. Recite together Proverbs 3:13-16 together.

History of Work

He who tills his land will have plenty of food,
but he who follows empty pursuits will have poverty in plenty.

Proverbs 28:19

There are many verses in Proverbs that talk about work ethic. Work ethic is the personal principles and character traits you display when you are working. For example, diligence and honesty would constitute a good work ethic while laziness and shoddy workmanship would make up a bad work ethic. Proverbs explores both good and bad habits in the work place.

The first thing you are going to look at concerning work is its history and origin. God assigned Adam work even in the Garden of Eden. In the perfect world before sin entered in, there was work to be done. Genesis 2:15 says God put the man into the garden to "cultivate it and _____ it."

His next job is found in Genesis 2:19-20 where Adam was assigned by God to name the animals. These jobs were issued even before Eve took that fateful bite. God created man to work.

When you think of work, do you immediately think of unpleasant tasks? I don't believe work has to be that way. Work is meaningful occupation of your time. I love to work hard physically. Give me a tree to dig up or a garage to build, and I am one happy woman. Some people prefer physical work and others mental work or social work. One kind of work is not better than another, although physical work does have added benefits such as a feeling of well- being because of chemical changes it sparks in your body and keeping your body in shape and healthy. Most of us will find that whatever jobs we undertake will be a combination of all three kinds of work.

God does not put a priority on kinds of work, but He does tell you in 2 Thessalonians 3:10-11 "If anyone is not willing to work, then he is not to _____ either. For we hear that some among you are leading an undisciplined life, doing no work at all, but acting like busybodies."

This is in line with Proverbs 28:19 at the beginning of your lesson. At the Jamestown settlement in Virginia in the 1600's, the common laborers were working and the gentry were playing. The leaders put this principle to work, and the gentry became productive citizens of the colony.

God does not require you to work all the time, for He set aside 1/7th of your time for rest. This is the purpose of the fourth commandment (Deuteronomy 5:12-13). "Observe the Sabbath day to _____ _____ _____ as the Lord your God commanded you. Six days you shall labor and do all your work, but the _____ day is a Sabbath of the Lord your God; in it you shall not do any work."

Many years ago in communist Russia, it was decided that men were wasting time and money by working six days and taking the seventh day off. The government decided to go to a ten-day work week with the eleventh day off. Production and morale went down and men became sick, and missed more days. They wisely went back to a seven-day week.[6] The God who created you for work also created you for rest.

Balance is the key. Proverbs 21:17 reminds you, "He who _____ _____ will become a poor man; He who loves wine and oil will not become rich."

This is not balance. Balance says he/she who works hard, plays hard. There is nothing wrong with well-earned rest. There is everything wrong with laziness and slackness on the job.

A practical principle is: When at work, work! When at play, play!

Remember you will get better at the activities you spend your time on. If you're balancing work and play 6:1, then you will be woman described in Proverbs 22:29: "Do you see a man skilled in his work? He shall stand before kings; He will not stand before obscure men." Remember work is meaningful occupation of your time. Work does not have to be an official job. Being a wife and a mom is meaningful work and a ministry.

What type of work do you like to do best? Physical, social, or mental? _____
What type of physical work do you do? _____
What type of social work do you do? _____
What type of mental work do you do? _____
What do you do for recreation? _____
What would you say your work to play ratio is? _____

Questions to think about:

1. Do you tend to be a workaholic or do you tend to avoid work as much as possible?

2. What motivates you to work hard?

3. Are you more valuable in God's estimation if you work hard or not?

Add Proverbs 3:17-18 to your memorized repertoire this week. Turn to Appendix A and underline or highlight the key words. You might also draw pictures or come up with actions.

Planning Ahead

Prepare your work outside
And make it ready for yourself in the field;
Afterwards then, build your house.

Proverbs 24:27

We talked before about having a plan for your money called a budget. It is also good to have a work plan so you are prepared for any contingencies which might occur.

Jesus is teaching in Luke 14:28-32 about salvation. He compares yielding all relationships and earthly possessions up to Him with two people who need to be wise planners.

Who are these two people?
1.
2.

The builder needs to have a plan before he builds, and the king should plan before he sends troops into battle. Jesus is saying that as Christians there will be a cost to discipleship as well. This cost is relinquishing your rights of relationship to others and to your possessions. This does not mean you are to live penniless and alone. Rather, as you turn all things over to Jesus, He changes your heart and gives you a new relationships and teaches you to use those relationships and your possessions for His kingdom. Whatever you turn over to Jesus, He turns back to you in wonderful ways—ways you may never dream but always for your good.

Just as the builder and the king should have a work plan, so should you. Your work plan might include college, learning a trade, trying a new business, or working two jobs for a time to save up for something big. There are long term plans and short term plans. Planning out your garden, or planning a meal would all be short term plans. Deciding on your educational track would be a longer term plan as well as deciding where marriage and children will fit into your life. The important thing is to *have* a plan. Count the costs.

Every decision you make will limit your later decisions. If you choose to go to medical school and finish six years of training, your choices have been limited to a career in the medical field. You would not be able to get a job as an engineer. If you decide to continue in the work which you are already doing, you limit your opportunities to move. Sometimes the plans are made for you if you get laid off or your company merges and moves to another city. God still has a plan even if the move is not your idea. Trust Him.

Commit each plan to the Lord asking for guidance, then go ahead and plan the best you can. Use the wisdom from Proverbs and the rest of Scripture to make biblical decisions. Sometimes God gives you the freedom to make choices. When a mom asks her child if he/she would like a chocolate chip cookie or an oatmeal cookie, she really doesn't care which he/she chooses. She will be happy with either choice. In the same way your Heavenly Father gives you choices that please Him. As long as you are not breaking the moral code of the Bible or a direct calling from God, you are free to choose. Using wisdom, talking to biblically wise people, praying, following your heart, looking at your aptitudes and desires should all give you clues to what some of your decisions should be.

Does God have a specific plan for your life? I believe He knows what choices you will make. He promises He will work all things out for your good (Romans 8:28), but He does not have a plan "A" and if you fail to find it, then you are living God's second best plan for your life. No, you are in a relationship with Christ. As you walk with Him, He will reveal to you if there is something specific you need to do. If not, then you are free to choose within His moral code. Note that in the Bible Abraham, Moses, and others were going about their business and God initiated the conversation leading to change.

1 Timothy 2:2 says, "To pray for those in authority so that we may lead a _____ and _____ life in all godliness and dignity."

Here are some practical questions you can ask yourself to help determine a course of action in any decision.
1. Does it follow God's moral code?
2. Is it something I have desired to do?
3. Does it fit into the pattern of things I have chosen to do in the past and have shown an aptitude for?
4. Will it lead me into a deeper relationship with Jesus?
5. What are my counselors, mentors, or other Christian leaders' ideas about this decision?
6. Have I prayed earnestly about this and feel free to make this decision?

If all these answers line up, then you are free to plan. Just remember no plan is set in stone and God often takes us down one path to get to a turn off for another direction. But until you feel God pulling you in a different direction, rest in your decision, enjoy the ride, and make sure you have counted the cost.

Psalm 138:8 says, "The Lord _____ _____what concerns me; Your lovingkindness, O Lord, is everlasting; Do not forsake the works of Your hands."

Don't fret and worry over decisions. Do as Philippians 4:6 says and know the peace of Philippians 4:7.

What does Philippians 4:6 tell you not to do? _____

What does this verse tell you to do? _____

What is the result from this obedience?_____

Questions to think about:

1. Are you successful at making a short term work plan and accomplishing it?

2. What is your long term work plan? Does it include college, a new job, marriage, children, retirement, ministry?

3. Are you making a plan through prayer and trusting God to lead, guide, and direct?

4. Work on memorizing Proverbs 3:17-18.

   How …
   And the …
   For her …
   And her …
   She is …
   And nothing …
   Long life …
   In her …
   Her ways are _____ ways
   And all her paths are _____.
   She is a tree of _____ to those who take hold of her,
   And happy are all who hold her_____.

Diligence

The hand of the diligent will rule,
But the slack hand will be put to forced labor.

Proverbs 12:24

Now that you have a plan, go forward with all diligence! The only way a plan can be successful is hard and diligent work. Proverbs has a lot to say about diligence and laziness.

Look up the following verses and dig up the joys of diligence. Make sure you read the whole verse.

Proverbs 10:4: "The hand of the diligent makes _____."

Proverbs 12:11: "He who tills his land will have plenty of _____."

Proverbs 12:14: "The _____ of a man's hands will return to him."

Proverbs 12:27: This verse implies that a diligent man will roast his _____. "The precious possession of a man is his _____."

Proverbs 13:4: "The _____ of the diligent is made fat."

Proverbs 14:23: "In all _____ there is profit."

Proverbs 27:18: "He who tends the fig tree will _____ its fruit, and he who cares for his master will be _____."

Proverbs 28:19: "He who tills his land will have plenty of _____, but he who follows empty pursuits will have poverty in plenty."

From these verses what would you say is the opposite of diligence? _____

It is very clear from these verses that not only will the diligent prosper, but the lazy will have want. Let's look at a few more verses.

Proverbs 27:23-27 is a warning. What is not forever? _____ This truth should move you to diligence.

Proverbs 12:11: Someone who pursues worthless things lacks what? _____

Proverbs 10:5: How will the son who sleeps in harvest act? _____

Proverbs 24:10: "If you are slack in the day of distress, your strength is _____."

Think about it. If you don't exercise and work out, you won't be ready for war. If you don't store up money or food for times of trouble, you won't have enough.

Proverbs 18:9: A slack person is considered a brother or kin to one whom? _____

Proverbs 20:13: What does a lazy person love? _____ What will this gain him?
_____

Proverbs 21:25-26: The result of a sluggard refusing to work is _____

Proverbs 20:4: Again, the sluggard does without because he will not _____

Proverbs 19:15: What will an idle man suffer? _____

Proverbs 10:26: A lazy person is going to find himself friendless and without a job because, "Like vinegar to the teeth and smoke to the eyes, so is the lazy one to those who send him."

How does vinegar taste? _____. Don't you want it far from you? This is how an employee looks at a lazy person. He is no good to the company, no good to himself, and no good to his family. Unfortunately, when someone chooses the path of laziness, they hurt others as well as themselves.

Look up two longer passages about a sluggard.

Read Proverbs 24:30-34.
Is your home clean? _____ Could it use some diligence? What about your car, work place, your other possessions?"

Proverbs 26:13-16.
Don't get into this bad habit of excuses! Do you really think there was a lion in the road? No, he was just lazy and didn't want to do what he was supposed to do, so he made up an excuse. If you do make up excuses, I hope they are better than these!

What is the sluggard compared to as he turns upon his bed? _____

That's a good comparison. You will notice a sluggard or lazy person has an awful lot of the traits of a biblical fool.

One of our favorite verses is Ecclesiastes 9:10. It's a great verse to memorize. "Whatever your hand finds to do, do it with all your might."

Questions to think about:

1. Are you an excuse maker?

2. What's the most creative excuse you ever made up or heard?

3. What areas do you need to become more diligent in?

4. Are you diligent in your relationships?

5. What might you commit to doing to become more diligent in these areas?

6. Work on your memory verses: Proverbs 3:13-18.

> How …
> And the …
> For her …
> And her …
> She is …
> And nothing …
> Long life …
> In her …
> Her _____ are _____ ways
> And all her _____ are _____.
> She is a _____ of _____ to those who take hold of her,
> And _____ are all who hold her _____.

God Promises the Holy Spirit

The crown of the wise is their riches,
But the folly of fools is their foolishness.

Proverbs 14:24

Let's talk about a very misunderstood and misused concept in church doctrine today. Many call it the "name it and claim it" doctrine. There are ministers in some churches and on the television teaching that if you have enough faith, and if you are living according to God's commandments, then all you have to do is ask for a material blessing, and God will give you whatever you want. They believe if your faith is strong enough then you can tap into God's resources at your discretion. There are many verses in the Bible they quote which can be used to support their doctrine if they don't take the whole context of Scripture to task.

For example, Luke 11:5-13 begins with the story of a person who has a friend stop by late at night. He doesn't have any bread to feed to this person, so he goes to another friend and asks for bread. This friend was already asleep and says, "Do not bother me." The parable goes on to say the sleeping friend will get up and give bread to his friend at the door not because of the friendship, but because of the persistence of the friend wanting the bread.

This parable is followed by a very well-known and often memorized verse. "So I say to you, ask, and it will be given to you; seek, and you will find; knock and it will be opened to you. For everyone who asks, receives; and he who seeks, finds; and to him who knocks, it will be opened." The very next verses say if a son asks a father for a fish, he won't give him a snake. If he asks for an egg, he won't give him a scorpion. This is followed by these words, "If you then, being evil, know how to give good gifts to your children, how much more will your heavenly Father give _____ _____ _____ to those who ask?"

The parables would lead you to think God is talking about meeting our material needs in the form of food. But He clearly states it is the Holy Spirit who will be given when asked.

Think back over history. There were many sincere, faithful, believing Christians during the first several hundred years of the church who were martyred for their faith. In American history some of the most faithful Christians were black slaves before and during the Civil War. There were Christians in Jerusalem when Titus overcame the town in 72 AD and starved the people. During the Boxer Rebellion in China, it was Christian missionaries who lost their lives. Did these faithful few not ask for God's provisions for food, protection, etc.? Was their faith not strong enough? Or were their deaths due to the sovereign plan of a sovereign God?

Jesus tells us that in this world there will be persecution but He will be there with us through them all in the form of the Holy Spirit, (Luke 11). There are many accounts of martyrs throughout history who died in fire or by sword or bullet who smiled, reached toward heaven, or sang praises as death encompassed them. The Holy Spirit was there and He was enough. He was the only bread and nourishment their souls needed.

So what does all of this have to do with Proverbs or work? Look again at the verse at the top of the lesson, Proverbs 14:24, "The crown of the wise is their riches, but the folly of fools is their foolishness." The riches that this and other verses refer to are the riches of His glory—His presence in a believer's life manifested by peace, love, joy, patience, kindness, goodness, faithfulness, gentleness, and self-control. These riches are stored up in heaven and are the riches you can have no matter what your earthly circumstances dictate. You are to work diligently to provide for your family, you are to pray to God for your daily bread, and you are to store up riches in heaven.

Look up these verses and see what they say about riches.

Proverbs 15:6: "Great wealth is in the house of the _____, but trouble is in the income of the wicked."

Notice wealth is contrasted with trouble. This wealth is the wisdom which comes from God and His Word.

Psalm 19:7-10: "The law of the Lord … the testimony of the Lord … The precepts of the Lord … the commandment of the Lord … the fear of the Lord … the judgments of the Lord … are more desirable than _____, yes, than much fine gold, Sweeter also than honey and the drippings of the honeycomb."

Let's review Proverbs 3:13-15: "How blessed is the man who finds _____ and the man who gains _____. For her profit is better than the profit of _____ and her gain better than fine _____. She is more precious than _____; and nothing you desire compares with her."

Any wealth which the righteous man, or Christian, has is because he applied wisdom to his situation, and God provided, and they were blessed. The absence of wealth does not dictate the absence of wisdom, righteousness, or faith. God's sovereignty and sovereign plan over mankind often means where there is a wealth of wisdom and faith, there is a lack of riches. God does promise to meet your basic needs if you ask. but you would be better served to ask for the Holy Spirit and His kingdom.

Questions to think about:

1. Have you ever felt that you did not have enough faith because God did not seem to answer your prayer?

2. What three answers might a parent or God give if you ask for something?

3. Describe a time when God told you no or to wait.

4. Say Proverbs 3:12-18.

> How …
> And the …
> For her…
> And her …
> She is …
> And nothing …
> Long life …
> In her …
> Her _____ are _____ _____
> And _____ her_____ are _____.
> She is a _____ of _____ to those who take _____ of her,
> And _____ are all who _____ her _____.

Wealth and Welfare

*He who oppresses the poor to make more for himself
Or who gives to the rich will only come to poverty.*

Proverbs 22:16

God's Word has much to say about the way we are to treat the poor. There may come a time in your life, even though you are working hard, when you won't have enough to meet the basic necessities of life. As I write this, the unemployment rate is 10.9, which is very high. Even many who are working have taken major pay cuts or are only working part-time jobs. Those with college degrees are vying for jobs which, normally, high school graduates would fill. By God's grace, my husband still has work. But there was a time when he couldn't find a job for about eight months. As I told you in a previous lesson, God provided miraculously during this time and our faith was strengthened. So, be thankful when you have plenty, realizing everything is from God's hand, be humble, and give to the poor.

1 Samuel 2:7 is a good reminder. "The Lord makes _____ and _____; He brings low, He also exalts."

Be careful of a judgmental attitude which may creep in when dealing with the poor. But also be discerning.

Psalm 82:3-4 tells you to "Vindicate the _____ and fatherless; do justice to the _____ and _____. Rescue the _____ and _____; Deliver them out of the hand of the wicked." The KJV says "Defend the poor and fatherless."

So you do have a responsibility to give to the poor. I would suggest that this is the poor who cannot help themselves due to age or disability, not those who are depending on government welfare due to laziness or habit. These you can best help by giving them job skills. The truly poor, especially orphans and widows, you should defend, provide for, and help. This year at Christmas our MOPS group (Mothers of Preschoolers) has adopted a family of a single mom and two small children. The mom is working and trying to provide, but there is just not enough to pay the monthly bills, let alone anything else.

Who do you know who is truly in need? _____ What might you do to help them out?
_____

Proverbs 22:22-23 says "Do not _____ the poor because he is poor, or _____ the afflicted at the gate; For the Lord will plead their case and take the life of those who rob them."

Not only are you to give to the poor, you are to be careful not to rob the poor. This would include making sure your business practices do not take from others who don't have. You are responsible for your money as well as your actions. Does your insurance company pay for abortions? Does the non-profit organization you support pay for drugs for the addicted? Does building a new high rise put people out of their homes? Does hiring an illegal alien for cheaper wages mean a legal citizen is out of work? God does care about your business practices. He promises to bless those who work righteousness.

Then there are the poor who are poor due to their choices, and Proverbs has something to say about them as well.

Proverbs 19:7 "All the _____ of a poor man hate him, how much more do his _____ abandon him!" This is a warning to keep you from wanting to be lazy and, thus, poor.

Back to God's economy of giving. Proverbs 11:24 says, "There is one who _____, and yet increases all the more, and there is one who _____ what is justly due, and yet it results only in want."

The world teaches that to have you must hoard and to give would leave you wanting, but God is sovereign and He says to give, and He will bring the increase. R.G. LeTourneau decided to test God on this principle. He decided to up his tithe to 90%, and to live off of 10%. He became a very successful business man inventing and patenting over 300 earth moving machines and he founded a Christian college and a camp and conference center. He had more than enough and gave most of his money away.[7] The Mayo brothers were doctors who founded the Mayo Clinics. They also were said to have given 50% of their income.[8]

Lastly, Proverbs has something to say about money gained by fraud.

Proverbs 13:11: "Wealth obtained by fraud _____, But the one who gathers by labor _____ it."

Proverbs 15:27: "He who profits _____ troubles his own house, but he who hates bribes will live."

Proverbs 11:18: "The wicked earns _____ wages, but he who sows righteousness gets a _____ reward."

Proverbs 10:2: "Ill-gotten gains do not profit, but righteousness delivers from _____."

That's God's perspective, again! What is riches compared to eternal damnation? Better the poor on earth who will live eternally with Jesus.

Proverbs 28:22: "A man with an evil eye hastens after wealth, and does not know that _____ will come upon him."

Proverbs 22:16: "He who oppresses the poor to make more for himself, or who gives to the _____ will only come to poverty."

A final encouragement: God says in Proverbs 13:22 "A good man leaves an inheritance to his children's children, and the wealth of the sinner is stored up for the righteous." God will take care of His own. Trust in Him to provide, but put your hand to the plow and you will live a life of great riches (stored up in heaven).

Questions to think about:

1. Are you tithing faithfully? _____ If not, will you trust God and begin today? God will be faithful and stretch your 90% to meet all your needs.

2. How might you give above your tithe?

3. Should you discern and treat differently the poor and the lazy poor? How might you treat each group to give the best help?

4. Recite Proverbs 3:1-18 aloud.

    How …
    And the …
    For her …
    And her …
    She is …
    And nothing …
    Long life …
    In her …
    Her ways …
    And all …
    She is …
    And all …

Week 3 Group Discussion

1. Do you tend to be a workaholic, or do you tend to avoid work as much as possible? (Matt. 21:28, Luke 5:5, John 5:17, Romans 16:6)

2. What motivates you to work hard?

3. Are you more valuable in God's estimation if you work hard or not? (Eph. 1:3-13, 2:4-10)

4. What are your long range plans? Does it include college, a new job, marriage, children, retirement, ministry?

5. What's the most creative excuse you ever made up or heard?

6. What areas do you need to become more diligent in? (Romans 12:8, 11, Heb. 6:11, Peter 1:5)

7. What might you commit to doing to become more diligent in these areas?

8. Have you ever felt you did not have enough faith because God did not seem to answer your prayer? (Ps. 3:4, 20:6, 34:4, 65:5)

9. Describe a time when God told you no or to wait.

10. Should you discern and treat differently the poor and the lazy poor? How might you treat each group to give the best help?

11. Recite Proverbs 3:13-18 together.

Wise Words I

Let the words of my mouth and the meditation of
My heart be acceptable in Your sight,
Oh, LORD, my rock and my Redeemer.

Psalm 19:14

Proverbs has a lot to say about the words you speak and the intentions of your heart. Actually, God addresses this issue throughout Scripture. Jesus speaks of the connection between the heart and the mouth in Matthew 12:34: "For the mouth speaks out of that which fills the _____."

He continues by explaining, "The good man brings out of his good treasure what is good; and the evil man brings out of his evil treasure what is evil." He sums it all up with these words: "But I tell you that every careless _____ that people speak, they shall give an accounting for it in the Day of Judgment. For by your _____ you will be justified, and by your _____ you will be condemned."

Your words must be awfully powerful! Your words are just a mirror of your heart. If you are seeking to live for Jesus, spending time in His Word, and trying to glorify God with your words and deeds, then your words will justify your hearts' intentions. If you are living for self, trying to get ahead even if you hurt others, looking out for number one, etc. your words will condemn those heart attitudes.

Circle the following statements which mirror a heart seeking to please God.

Well done!   You are so special to me   I love you

Way to go!   Can't you do anything right?   I am God's precious child

I can't believe you did that, you moron!   I am no good.   You idiot!

Make sure your words to yourself and others are truth–biblical truth. God thinks you are a delight, and He loves you!

You will need to work on memorizing Proverbs 18:21. This is a key verse. Write this verse out. _____

_____

_____

What does it mean that life and death are in the power of the tongue? Those are very strong words! What God is telling you is you can offer words of encouragement which will lead to life for your listener, or you can speak words of death by degrading your listener. Remember words are spoken not just to others, but to yourself as well. What does your self-talk look like? Are you speaking works of life or death to yourself? Satan is ever the deceiver and will put words into your head. He doesn't speak in third person "You are no good!", but rather in first person, "I am no good. God can't love me." This is why 2 Corinthians 10:5 tells us to, "Take every thought captive to the obedience of Christ." In other words, look at every word you speak or think and make sure they line up with the Word of God.

God says you are the Apple of His Eye (Zech. 2:8). He is speaking to the Jewish nation, but as children grafted in (Rom. 11:17), it includes us. You are fearfully and wonderfully made (Ps. 139:14). If Satan is telling you otherwise, it is time to tell Satan to take a hike! You must be in the Word to know what God thinks about you. Then don't let anyone or Satan tell you otherwise!

"If abortion had been legal, I would have aborted you." Your son will never be handsome; he has a big head like you." "It's a good thing you had boys, you would have been a terrible mother to girls." These were all words from my mother to me. They were words of death which held me back for years from being able to find joy and contentment in spite of being a Christian.

What death words were spoken to you that you are still believing? _____

_____

Proverbs speaks so much about the tongue for good and evil that you are going to make a chart contrasting the two. Then we will tear what we learn apart and look at some specific uses of the tongue God says is fit only for the fool!

Use the chart below and on the following pages to list what each verse says about the tongue, words, lies, etc. Place your answer under the correct heading.

	<u>Righteous man</u>	<u>Biblical Fool</u>
Prov. 10:6		
10:10		
10:11		
10:14		

10:18

10:19

10:20

10:21

10:31

10:32

Questions to think about:

1. What sin of the tongue stands out most to you?

2. Why is this a sin? How does it go against who God is?

3. Is your self-talk defeating you or bringing you victory? (I had a counselor put a rubber band on my wrist. Every time I caught myself being negative with my thoughts towards myself, I was to tweak it. I was wounded by the end of a week!)

Start adding Proverbs 3:19-20 to your memorized passage. Turn to Appendix A and underline or highlight key words. You might also draw or act out the verses.

Wise Words II

With his mouth the godless man destroys his neighbor,
But through knowledge the righteous will be delivered.

Proverbs 11:9

Continue your chart from yesterday.

	Righteous Man	Biblical Fool
Prov. 11:9		
11:13		
12:6		
12:13		
12:14		
12:22		
12:25		
13:2		
13:3		
13:5		
14:3		

14:5

14:23

14:25

15:1

15:2

15:4

15:7

15:14

15:23

15:26

15:28

16:13

16:21

16:23

16:24

16:28

17:7

17:9

17:14

17:20

17:28

Questions to think about:

1. What sin of the tongue stands out most to you?

2. Why is this sin? How does it go against who God is?

3. Work on saying Proverbs 3:13-20.

> How …
> And the …
> For her …
> And her …
> She is …
> And nothing …
> Long life …
> In her …
> Her ways …
> And all …
> She is …
> And all …
> The Lord by wisdom founded the_____,
> By understanding He established the _____.
> By His knowledge the _____ were broken up
> And the skies drip with _____.

Wise Words III

The words of a man's mouth are deep waters;
The fountain of wisdom is a bubbling brook.

Proverbs 18:4

$\mathcal{F}$inish the chart.

	<u>Righteous Man</u>	<u>Biblical Fool</u>
Prov. 18:4		
18:6		
18:7		
18:8		
18:13		
18:20		
18:21		
19:1		
19:5		
19:9		
19:22		

19:28

20:15

20:17

20:19

20:20

20:25

21:6

21:23

21:28

22:10

22:11

22:14

23:15-16

24:28-29

25:11

25:12

25:13

25:14

25:15

25:18

25:23-24

26:2

26:18-19

26:20

26:21

26:23

26:24

26:25

26:28

28:23

29:8

29:20

Questions to think about:

1. What sin of the tongue stands out most to you?

2. Why is this sin? How does it go against who God is?

3. How does your mouth compare?

4. Are your words wounding others and yourself or giving grace to others and yourself?

5. Work on memorizing Proverbs 3:13-20.

> How …
> And the …
> For her …
> And her …
> She is …
> And nothing …
> Long life …
> In her …
> Her ways …
> And all …
> She is …

And all …
The Lord by _____ founded the _____,
By _____ He established the _____.
By His _____ the _____ were broken up
And the skies _____ with _____.

The Tongue Can't Be Tamed

The one who guards his mouth preserves his life;
The one who opens wide his lips comes to ruin.

Proverbs 13:3

The book of James has a lot to say about the tongue. James 3:1 starts by warning teachers that they will incur a stricter judgment. When you take a position of authority, you are accountable to God for every word which proceeds from your mouth. Who are you teaching? _____ (It may be a child, grandchild, friend, etc.) Are your words leading them closer to God's truth? Are your words bringing life?

James 3:2 continues, "For we all stumble in many ways. If anyone does not stumble in what he says, he is a _____ man, able to bridle the whole body as well." The Hebrew for *perfect* depicts a mature man making this not an impossible statement, but rather a goal to reach.

The tongue is compared to what three items in James 3:3-6?
   1.
   2.
   3.

How much power over the rest of the body do these verses say the tongue has? _____

James 3:8 sums up these verses. "But no one can tame the tongue; it is a restless evil and full of deadly poison." It seems as if the tongue is without restraint.

James is actually setting you up for his admonishment found in verses 9-10. "From the same mouth come both _____ and _____. My brethren, these things ought not to be this way."

James continues by asking couple of questions which answers are unmistakable in verses 11-12. "Does a fountain send out from the same opening both _____ and _____ water? Can a fig tree, my brethren, produce _____, or a vine produce _____? Nor can salt water produce fresh." The answers are a resounding "No!"

James then turns the conversation making it personal. He asks, "Who among you is wise and understanding? Let him show by his good behavior his _____ in the gentleness of wisdom."

James links the words of your mouth to the condition of your heart. Luke 6:45 says, "The good man out of the good treasure of his heart brings forth what is _____; and the evil man out of the evil treasure brings forth what is _____; for his mouth speaks from that which fills his heart."
Looking at your words, what is the condition of your heart? _____

Finally, read James 3:17-18. List the characteristics of God's wisdom.

1.   6.
2.   7.
3.   8.
4.   9.
5.

Are these characteristics of your mouth? _____ If not, pray that God would begin to cleanse you of evil thoughts and help you to grow in these fruits. Fruit doesn't grow by force or wishful thinking. Fruit grows when the roots are in deep, nutritious dirt with access to water and the limbs are raised to the sun. In the same way, you can grow in spiritual fruits by putting your roots deep into the Word of God with access to the Holy Spirit and raise your arms to the Son in worship and praise.

Read the following verses and notice the relationship between the tongue and the heart.

Proverbs 10:20: "The _____ of the righteous is as choice silver, the _____ of the wicked is worth little."

Proverbs 10:31: "The _____ of the righteous flows with wisdom, but the perverted _____ will be cut out".

Proverbs 15:28: "The _____ of the righteous ponders how to answer, but the _____ of the wicked pours out evil things."

Proverbs 22:11: "He who loves purity of _____ and whose _____ is gracious the king is his friend."

Proverbs 23:15-16: "My son, if your _____ is wise, my own heart also will be glad; and my inmost being will rejoice when your _____ _____ what is right."

Proverbs 26:24: "He who hates disguises it with his _____, but he lays up deceit in his _____."

In these following verses notice the relationship between knowledge (of God's Word and way) and the mouth of the foolish.

Proverbs 11:9: "With his _____ the godless man destroys his neighbor, but through _____ the righteous will be delivered."

Proverbs 10:14: "Wise men store up _____, but with the _____ of the foolish, ruin is at hand."

Questions to think about:

1. What does your tongue say about your heart?

2. What is the relationship between knowledge and the tongue?

3. If you are having a hard time taming your tongue, what should your approach be to getting it under control?

4. Let the words of your mouth be Proverbs 3:1-20. Recite it out loud.

> How …
> And the …
> For her …
> And her …
> She is …
> And nothing …
> Long life …
> In her …
> Her ways …
> And all …
> She is …
> And all …
> The _____ by _____ founded the _____,
> By_____ He _____ the _____.
> By His _____ the _____ were _____
> _____ And the _____ _____ with _____.

Last Word–Lying

Lying lips are an abomination to the Lord,
But those who deal faithfully are His delight.

Proverbs 12:22

Lying lips are an abomination to the Lord. Why does lying offend God so greatly that He says in Proverbs 10:31, "The perverted tongue will be cut out."? Lies are the opposite of truth. Truth is the essence of the character of God. God's holiness demands truth and purity. Look at a few more verses in Proverbs and find out God's thoughts on lies.

Proverbs 12:19: "Truthful lips will be _____ forever, but a lying tongue is only for a _____."

Proverbs 17:7: "Excellent speech is not fitting for a _____, much less are lying lips to a prince."

Proverbs 21:6: "The acquisition of treasures by a lying tongue is a _____ _____ the pursuit of _____."

God's arch enemy, Satan, is known as the Father of lies (John 8:44). You will find three weapons which Satan uses in 2 Corinthians 10:5.

1. Speculations – These are the lies saying that if you could do something over again, you would, and if you had done things differently life would be much better. They are the *What if's,* the *If only's,* the *I should have's.* When these words are floating around in your mind, they should be red flags signaling that Satan is putting lies in your heart. Speculating is not reality. It is not truth.

2. Pride – Every lofty thing raised up against the knowledge of God.

3. Lies – Things raised up against the knowledge of God. God's knowledge is truth, anything against truth is a lie.

The good news is you can destroy these weapons of Satan by replacing the lies with the Truth. John 8:31-32 claims the, "Truth will set you _____." Free from Satan's grasp, his influence, his lies.

1 John 2:16 tells you lies can also originate from Satan's domain—the world which you live in and your own mind. What is a lie the world is proclaiming?_____

Your answer might have been, "Only the pretty are lovely", "You should only take care of yourself", or "Drinking beer and having sex will make you popular."

Satan can't create. He, himself, is a created being. Instead, you will find him imitating God's creation and perverting it with his lies. Music was created by God for worship, Satan's music brings people into bondage. God created sex for an intimate and right relationship within marriage, Satan has perverted sex to becoming vulgar and leading people away from marital commitments.

Another lie from Satan is accusations and false guilt. You must know the truth of Jesus' sacrifice, your justification, your adoption, your reconciliation, and your sanctification. Then you can recognize Satan's lies and fight against them.

There are also lies of your own mind or flesh. Your flesh is your own unique version of meeting God-given needs in your own way, using your own strength and your own resources apart from God. Flesh might look good—joining the marines, having a large family, having a great career, etc., but if the motivation for these things is getting approval or being loved, then they are of the flesh. Flesh can also look putrid—drugs, sex, perfectionism, work holism, manipulations, neediness, etc.

For a list of the flesh and an inventory to identify your flesh, you can go to my website *www.abidingtruthministry. com.* Click on Resources, then go to Conference Notes. You will find the Flesh Inventory under *What Really Happened at the Cross.*[9]

Even if flesh looks good, remember your best is as filthy rags (Isaiah 64:6). Just because vomit is tied up in a pretty package with a big bow, it is not righteous. Anything you do apart from God is flesh. Look up John 5:15: "Apart from _____ you can do nothing."

You fight lies in your mind which were planted there from others. We all have these old tapes running through our minds. Whether it was a critical parent, a demeaning teacher, or careless children, these tapes can run forever unless they are captured when they come to mind and applied to the truth. It is sometimes helpful to remind yourself, "That was then, this is now."

You are told in 2 Corinthians 10:3-4 that you are not in a battle of the flesh, but a spiritual battle. Ephesians. 6:12 reiterates this: "For our struggle is not against flesh and blood, but against the _____, against the _____, against the _____ _____ of this darkness, against the _____ _____ of wickedness in the heavenly places.

In his commentary series, *Thru the Bible,* J. Vernon McGee speculates on the demonic rulers mentioned here.

He says rulers or principalities are demons with oversight of nations (see Daniel). Powers are demons wanting to possess humans. World forces of this darkness are demons with charge over Satan's worldly business. And Spiritual forces of wickedness in the heavenly places are demons in charge over false religions.[10]

Trying to fight a spiritual battle in the flesh leads to despair (Romans 7:15-8:1). The only way to be victorious is to reckon the flesh dead and yield to God (Romans 6:11).

God doesn't leave you defenseless. What are your weapons listed in Ephesians 6:10-18?
1.
2.
3.
4.
5.
6.
7.

These weapons are powerful for the destruction of fortresses in spiritual realm and in the physical realm. But you must do what Ephesians 6: 11 commands you to do. What is this command? _____

_____

Your life must be lined up with the Word of God. If you are disobeying the Commander, then you have stepped out from under His protection.

The battle plan has four steps.
1. Recognize the lie
2. Replace with truth (Philippians 4:8)
3. Reckon yourself dead to the power of sin (Romans 6:11)
4. Rest (Isaiah 30:15)

There is a principle which says: What you believe, you will think about; what you think about, you will feel; what you feel, you will act upon. If you are believing a lie, then you will think about it, feel as if this lie is true, and act upon it detrimentally to yourself and others. Rather you should believe truth, think truth, feel truth, and act upon truth.

For a deeper study about lies, you might want to check out these books:
The Lies We Believe by Dr. Chris Thurman[11]
The Lies Women Believe: And the Truth That Sets Them Free by Linda L. DeMoss[12]
Praying God's Word: Breaking Free from Spiritual Strongholds by Beth Moore[13]
Search for Significance: Seeing Your True Worth Through God's Eyes by Dr. Robert McGee[14]
The Confident Woman: Knowing Who You Are in Christ by Anabel Gilliam[15]

Questions to Think About:

1. Does lying come easily for you?

2. Is any lying justifiable?

3. What lies are you believing?

4. What is the truth about your justification? (Rom. 3:24, 28 5:1)

5. What is the truth about your adoption? (Rom. 8:15, 23, Eph. 1:5)

6. What is the truth about your reconciliation? (Rom. 5:10, 2 Cor. 5:18, 20)

7. What is the truth about your sanctification? (1 Cor. 1:2, 6:11)

8. Recite Proverbs 3:13-20 by memory.

> How …
> And the …
> For her …
> And her …
> She is …
> And nothing …
> Long life …
> In her …
> Her ways …
> And all …
> She is …
> And all …
> The Lord …
> By understanding …
> By His …
> And the …

Week 4 Group Discussion

1. What sins of the tongue stood out most to you?

2. How do these sins go against who God is? (1 Peter 1:15-16)

3. How does your mouth compare to the righteous man's mouth?

4. Is your self-talk pleasing to God?

5. What is the relationship between your heart and your tongue? (Matt. 12:34)

6. What is the relationship between knowledge and your tongue? (Prov. 2:6, 15:2, 15:4)

7. If you are having a hard time taming your tongue, what should your approach be to getting it under control?

8. Is any lying justifiable? (Ps. 25:5, 10, 26:3, John 8:3214:6, 1 John 1:6, 8, 2:4)

9. What lies are you believing?

10. Recite Proverbs 3:13-20 together.

Destructive vs. Constructive Anger

He who is slow to anger has great understanding,
But he who is quick-tempered exalts folly.

Proverbs 14:29

This verse has a partner verse in the New Testament: James 1:19-20. You are to "Be quick to
_____, slow to _____, and slow to _____, because
the anger of man does not work the righteousness of God!"

Anger is the natural response you have towards being hurt whether it is an emotional hurt or a physical hurt.
The old saying, "Sticks and stones may break my bones, but words will never hurt me," is as false as anything.
Words can hurt and do hurt. Whether the anger comes from abuse, a misunderstanding, or expectations which
are too high, anger is a gift from God.

Now, you are thinking, "What! How is this rage and desire to get even, this hurt and depression, this
overwhelming need to cry and to be understood from God?" We were made in God's image. God has emotions
(compassion, anger, love, etc.), so His creation does as well. Emotions, in and of themselves, are not good or
bad. How you choose to respond to your emotions can be a problem however.

Anger is a warning sign to you that you have been hurt or disrespected. Anger is a neutral emotion which
comes from God. Even God gets angry, so the anger is not the problem. When you allow anger to become sin,
you have a problem. Anger is an emotional reaction which comes in the face of hurt. By expressing the anger
someone feels toward someone or something, most people are standing up for themselves. They are trying to
drive home the idea that they deserve to be treated correctly. Anger is a way of saying "Notice my needs!"

God created within each of us two needs: the need for love and affirmation. We all need to feel worthy and
significant. When these needs are not being met or are being threatened, we get angry. Anger can start out as a
signal and a method of self-preservation, but turn into a pattern of destruction. This destruction can be turned
on others or ourselves.

Look at Ephesians 4:26. Anger is neither good nor bad. This verse says, "Be angry, but _____ not."

The anger is not the problem; how you handle your anger can be. Use your anger as a positive motivator in giving one another feedback about how life can be lived more productively. In other words, communicate why you are angry and help to come up with a plan to solve the problem which led to the anger. There are two ways to communicate your anger: destructively and constructively.

Let's look at a chart of these two responses. With Dr. Les Carter's permission, the following information came from his book, *The Anger Workbook*.[16]

Destructive or aggressive anger	**Constructive or assertive anger**
Seeks to punish person	Seeks to help person who does wrong
Does not care about the other person's point of view.	Tries to be understanding
Is stubborn, immovable, and demanding.	Is flexible and willing to seek alternatives.
Is condemning and judgmental.	Recognizes we all have faults.
Has high expectations of everyone.	Knows even the finest people sometimes make mistakes.
Cares about what happens to oneself.	Cares about the welfare of others.
Holds grudges.	Knows the value of forgiving.
Does not notice one's own areas of weaknesses.	Recognizes that one can always improve.[17]

Use your anger to solve a problem; don't escalate the situation with unwise words or actions. Think first, speak second

Here are a few good ideas to practice when communicating.
Before you communicate:
1. Do not attempt to establish your own superiority.
2. Make sure anger is constructive.
3. Be aware of responsiveness of recipient.
4. Consider feelings and circumstances of recipient (timing is everything)!

As you communicate:

1. Discriminate essential from non-essential problems.
2. Confront problems as soon as possible.
3. Stick to the subject.
4. Be honest about your feelings (I statements).
5. Avoid terms of exaggeration.
6. Refrain from character assassination.
7. Listen to understand.
8. Give yourself a time limit. (Don't carry on 2 hour lectures!)
9. Don't ask loaded questions.
10. Keep a positive attitude,
11. Be tactful about when and where.
12. Remember winning is not the goal.[87]

Proverbs 12:18 will help you to remember to control your angry responses. "There is one who speaks _____ like the thrusts of a sword, but the tongue of the wise brings _____."

Tomorrow's lesson will give you some practical steps for using your anger productively.

Questions to think about:

1. On a scale of 1-10, what is your anger level?

2. Do you tend to confront the things which make you angry or repress your anger and hurt?

3. Practice some pretend situations which would make you angry and role play aggressive behavior and assertive behavior. This could be done in your family as well. Take turns coming up with scenarios.

Turn to Appendix A and add verses 21-22 to your repertoire. Underline or highlight key words. You might also want to draw or act out the verses.

Steps to Controlling Anger

A quick-tempered man acts foolishly,
And a man of evil devices is hated.

Proverbs 14:17

Yesterday you learned that anger is not sin, but what you do with your anger can be, so how do you control your anger?

1. You need to acknowledge the hurt. Pain, hurt, and anger are real and it is good to admit these things and the depth of the hurt. Find someone who you can talk to—a friend or a Christian counselor who will listen and give godly feedback.

2. Secondly, you must grieve the hurt. Give yourself permission to be sad about the loss or hurt whether it is a loss of relationship, respect, or circumstance. The hurt is real and you need time to work through the grief process. For me this also often includes a physical release through walking or shooting baskets, etc.

3. You must give your hurt to God even if it is God at whom you are angry. He is big enough to handle your anger. Let Him know, and talk to Him. God is the God of comfort (2 Corinthians 1:3-5). We will talk about forgiveness tomorrow, but remember God has forgiven you and requires you to forgive others. God is bigger than any circumstance. He will carry it for you.

   Read 1 Peter 5:6-7: "Therefore humble yourselves under the _____ hand of God, that He may exalt you at the proper time, casting all your anxiety on Him, because He _____ for you."

   Matthew 11:28 carries a great promise. Write this promise here._____
   _____

4. You must release the person whom you are angry with to God for "Vengeance is Mine!' thus saith the Lord." (Deuteronomy 32:35 KJV).

5. You are ready to speak rationally. This might include strategizing how you can react differently next time, resetting of healthy boundaries, or time and place and heart of confrontation.

Steps for working with angry children are:

1. Allow for a physical release with boundaries (Ex. You may run around the block or shoot baskets. You may not hit, punch, kick, or be disrespectful.)

2. Allow for an emotional release verbally with boundaries. (Ex. You may state how you feel, but you may not be disrespectful. You may talk, you may not yell.)

3. Discuss rationally the wrong done. (How much of it was the child's fault? How could they have reacted differently? Was the truth told? Is the anger because of feeling disrespect or unloved? etc.)

4. Lead them to repentance if necessary for their part and to forgiveness for the other person's part.

5. Decide if new boundaries need to be set on this relationship.

What happens when you don't follow these steps and you let anger reign in your heart? Anger can turn into bitterness, then into malice, then wrath, hatred, revenge, and eventually lead to multiple problems like destructive behavior, psychosomatic illness, suicidal ideation, and depression (Col. 3:8).

Bitterness is "characterized by intense antagonism or hostility,"[19] according to *Dictionary.com*. Bitterness is like drinking poison and hoping the other person will die from it. Bitterness hurts only you not the object of your hurt or pain. The writer of Hebrews warns you about not letting bitterness take root in your life. Hebrews 12:15 says, "See to it that no one comes short of the grace of God: that no root of _____ springing up causes trouble, and by it many be defiled." When this root takes hold, it is painful but necessary to dig it up. It would be better to deal with your anger before it can lead to bitterness.

What trouble might follow?
    Malice – the desire to harm others or do mischief; evil intent
    Wrath – violent anger; fury
    Hatred – seething fury turned towards the destruction of another
    Revenge – actually carrying out the evil intents of the heart

Yes, anger is best dealt with quickly. Read Ephesians 4:26-27, "Be angry, and yet do not sin; do not let the _____ _____ _____ on your anger, and do not give the devil an opportunity."

If you are suffering from destructive behavior, psychosomatic illness (migraines, anorexia, tiredness, etc.), suicidal thoughts, or depression, then it is likely your emotional bucket is full and overflowing. Let me explain. We all have a capacity for emotions—our emotional bucket. If you allow the emotions of the past to fill up this bucket because you have not resolved them, then something relatively minor might happen, and all of the sudden your bucket tips over and you are like an angry volcano spewing forth all the pent up anger and hurt. You need to keep your bucket empty, so you have reserve emotional space when there is a new hurt.

For me to empty my bucket, I had to go back to things which happened a long time ago because I had repressed those memories and feelings. Just by talking them through, choosing to give them to Jesus and letting Him be the Lord of my past and forgiving those who had hurt me, my bucket got empty, and oh, the joy that swept in and filled me up! The sun was brighter and the circumstances in my life became clearer and the people dearer! Now I keep my emotional bucket close to empty by talking things out as they happen. Express your anger by communicating effectively and constructively and then releasing it.

On the following picture of a train engine and a caboose you see the word *Emotions* in the engine with *Truth of God's Word* following behind. What's wrong with this picture? _____

_____

There's going to be a train wreck! In this next picture the word *Emotions* is behind the engine and *Truth of God's Word* is leading the way. Now you will get there! God's Word lasts forever; your emotions come and go, and come and go! Don't let your emotions lead you or drive you, rather hold tight to the Word of God, believe His promises even when they don't seem to be true, and give Him thanks and praise. Your emotions will get on board. Let your emotions be the warning light to make you stop and think about what was said and done, but then react as God would have you.

Often the key to getting over a bad mood or depression is to sing praises. It's hard to keep frowning when you are thankful for what God has done. Give it a try!

Questions to think about:

1. How do you grieve the hurts of your life?

2. How full or empty is your emotional bucket?

3. What pulls your train—your emotions or God's Word?

4. Fill in the blanks for Proverbs 3:1-22.

> How …
> And the …
> For her …
> And her …
> She is …
> And nothing …
> Long life …
> In her …
> Her ways …
> And all …
> She is …
> And all …
> The Lord …
> By understanding …
> By His …
> And the …
> My son, let them not vanish from your _____;
> Keep sound wisdom and _____,
> So they will be life to your _____
> And adornment to your _____.

Choosing Forgiveness

There is a way which seems right to a man,
But its end is the way of death.

Proverbs 14:12

This verse can apply to many things in your life, but it definitely is true about whether to hold a grudge and become bitter or to forgive. The world says to stay angry; you have that right. But Jesus says we are to forgive one another (Matthew 6:14). Let's look at this verse a little closer.

Matthew 6:14-15: "For if you forgive others for their transgressions, your heavenly Father _____ also forgive you. But if you do not forgive others, then your Father _____ _____ forgive your transgressions."

That's something to think about. On a scale from 1 – 10, how important is it to God that you forgive others?
1   2   3   4   5   6   7   8   9   10 (circle a number: 1–not very important to 10–very important.)

That's right, a 10! Matthew 6:14-15 can be a little confusing because you received forgiveness of all of your sins when Jesus died on the cross for you, and you chose to believe in Him and be born again. I believe what this is saying is when you became born again and received the Holy Spirit into your life, you received the power and desire necessary to forgive others. If you don't want to forgive, then you haven't truly experienced God's forgiveness.

Remember the parable of the king in Matthew 18:23-35? He forgave a man a great debt, but that man turned to his neighbor who owed him little and demanded repayment. When he couldn't pay he threw him in prison. The king then came to the first man, and he was handed over to the torturers with these words: "Should you not also have had mercy on your fellow slave, in the same way that I had mercy on you?" Then Jesus adds to this parable: "My heavenly Father will also do the same to you if each of you does not forgive his brother from your heart."

Forgiveness is a journey. Remember the train in yesterday's lesson? You must first turn over the anger to God and stand on His Word. He will comfort you. You must believe everyone will be punished in the end who has not confessed Jesus as Lord. God can handle the vengeance part; you are to forgive. The emotions will follow as you ask God for wisdom and strength to forgive someone who has hurt you. There was a time in my life where I forgave someone who had hurt me very deeply. I told God every day for months that I had forgiven her. But I still cried every time I said her name. I didn't feel like I had forgiven her. Forgiveness starts with a volitional decision to forgive. The you must turn your emotions over to God and let Him heal you.

Through time, my heart turned tender towards this person, and I knew God had done a work in my heart and forgiveness was complete and the hurt had healed. Eventually, God called on me to go back into a relationship with this person, love her, and to be her friend. I was able to do so joyfully, but cautiously at first. Now I can wholeheartedly serve this person and love and accept her.

There are others I have chosen to forgive, but also chose not to go back into relationship with because there has been no change in their hearts. I don't deserve their abuse and choose to move on.

This is important. You might want to highlight it. Forgiveness is not about not having negative emotions about someone, or about having good feelings about someone, but rather releasing them from an obligation for a debt.

Forgiveness is not an emotion; it is a choice of your will.

When something happens and you have been hurt and are angry, you might say something like, "Boy, she sure owes me an apology!" There is a debt there. You feel that the one who wronged you owes you to make it right. Forgiveness is canceling this debt and setting the other person free. This does not mean there shouldn't be boundaries put on the relationship, but it does mean healthy, honest communication.

Forgiveness does not require an apology. There comes a time when you need to forgive someone whom you cannot confront because of death or because of the other person's anger. In times like these it is helpful to either write a letter to the person, pouring out the depth of the hurt and the fact that you have chosen to forgive, or find a friend or counselor to talk through the pain and hurt. Let them know you are choosing forgiveness. You don't have to mail the letter. Show it to a friend, talk it out with a counselor, and then burn it or rip it up. I taught a group of ladies who were in a Bible study because of abuse in their pasts who wrote the name of their abuser on a helium balloon and released it to God. As we watched those balloons soar away, we were able to let go of the hurt, forgive our abusers, give it to God and begin to heal.

Forgiveness requires a humbling of the heart—a recognizing of your guilt before the Lord. Even as a Christian, I struggled with this because I was and had always been a fairly good person. By man's standards, I wasn't so bad. A lot of my anger was because I had been the victim. When I got serious about dealing with my past, God humbled my heart and showed me my sins, my sinful attitudes, my self-reliance, etc. With this humbling came a greater appreciation for what Christ had done for me. He, too, had been a victim, but He forgave and demands that you, too, forgive.

Les Carter and Frank Minirth have written several helpful books on forgiveness. Two of these are: *Choosing to Forgive*[20] and *The Forgiveness Workbook*.[21] With Dr. Carter's permission, the following ideas and tomorrow's lists are from these books.

Forgiveness is the willingness to let go of self-harming or ineffective forms of anger, choosing instead to turn over the ultimate resolution of the wrong to God.

Forgiveness is the act of setting someone free from an obligation to you that is a result of wrong doing against you.[21]

Tomorrow you will look at excuses people give not to forgive and what forgiveness does and doesn't mean.

Questions to think about:

1. Is there anyone you need to forgive? Who?

2. What debt will you have to forgive in order to forgive this person?

3. How much did God forgive you? For what attitudes and actions has God forgiven you?

4. What excuses do you give for not forgiving?

5. Keep memorizing! Proverbs 3:13-22.

> How …
> And the …
> For her …
> And her …
> She is …
> And nothing …
> Long life …
> In her …
> Her ways …
> And all …
> She is …
> And all …
> The Lord …
> By understanding …
> By His …
> And the …
> My son, let them not _____ from your _____;
> Keep sound _____ and _____,
> So they will be _____ to your _____
> And _____ to your _____.

Week 5 / Day 4

Reasons Not to Forgive

A joyful heart makes a cheerful face,
But when the heart is sad, the spirit is broken.

Proverbs 15:13

Nothing will make a heart sad and break the spirit like unforgiveness. Remember, if you don't forgive, then bitterness will take root in your heart, and bitterness is like a poison to your soul.

Yesterday you also learned that if you don't forgive others, then God won't forgive you. He wants you to be free from bitterness and anger, so you might be able to lead a cheerful and joyful life.

Now, you are going to look at some lists from Les Carter's books about excuses people give not to forgive.

Reasons people won't forgive:

1. "I'd just be sending the message that he/she can do wrong and get away with it."
2. "This would mean I've got to bury my anger."
3. If I forgive it means the other person wins and I lose."
4. "I guess I'll just have to put a smile on my face and say everything's all right."
5. "I feel that I'm being required to go soft on something that's severely wrong."
6. "One more time I've got to play the good-guy role while the bad guys just skip on their way."[22]

Numbers one and five put the person in the place of judge and jury over the wrong doer taking on the responsibility to make sure the person is judged and can't just get away with it. There are times you need to tell someone in authority about someone's actions because these actions will put this person in further danger to themselves or others. These circumstances would include knowing an underage person is drinking alcohol or doing drugs, someone is doing something illegal, cutting or threatening suicide, putting others at danger, perhaps reckless driving, etc. If any of these situations is the case, then you have a duty to that person to seek out their authority or friends and let them know. But your communication should be constructive, not vindictive. Forgive that person, feel sorry for that person, and let God do a work in their lives. It is not your responsibility.

Numbers two and four deal with repressing or burying anger. This is not properly handling anger. Ignoring anger won't make it go away! Release your anger through the steps we set out in the lesson on day two of this week. Put it behind you and look ahead. If you bury it or repress it, it will come back and haunt you!

Look at Philippians 3:13-14. "Brethren I do not regard myself as laying hold of it yet; but one thing I do: _____ what lies behind and reaching forward to what lies ahead, I press on toward the goal for the prize of the upward call of God in Christ Jesus."

For years, I thought this meant literally to forget the hurts of the past and move on. I tried for 25 years to keep looking forward and to press on. I made a lot of headway, but there was always a discontent and depression lurking in my heart. When I faced my past and forgave those who had hurt me, then I could truly put it behind and move on. Before, I was not forgetting so much as burying, repressing, ignoring it. Forgetting is in the progressive tense which means you are to be about forgetting. If the hurt were a big bonfire, you would turn your back to it and begin walking, running, or crawling away from it. As long as you are making progress away from it, then you are forgetting.

Numbers three and six are martyr's excuses. Poor me! I always have to say I am sorry first! He wins, I lose! The good guy (me) gets the shaft! Okay, this may all be true, but God says you are to humble yourself, serve others, and forgive. This won't make you a lesser person, but a bigger man (or woman)! You don't lose; you win with a heart at peace with God. The circumstances may make others think the other person won, but eventually, as you walk around cheerful and joyful and the other person is full of remorse and hate, they will realize you are the true winner! And if not, that's okay too, because you should be about pleasing God, not man.

Read 2 Corinthians 5:9-10.
What should your ambition be? _____
Who will appear before the judgment seat? _____
What will be judged there? _____

As a Christian, you will be allowed into the kingdom of God (heaven), but there is also a judgment for you according to your deeds. You will be given crowns based upon your motives and deeds that you, in turn, will place before Jesus. I don't have time here to go into this study, but there are five crowns mentioned in the New Testament. You may enjoy researching this further on your own.

I would add one more excuse to the list above. "He or she didn't apologize or ask for my forgiveness." Yes, it's easier to forgive when the other person realizes the hurt they've caused and apologizes, but Jesus died for you while you were yet a sinner (Romans 5:8)! Sometimes the person who hurt you won't ask for forgiveness. At times like this, you must remember that you forgive in obedience to God and to keep your own heart from bitterness. Unforgiveness is like eating a poison apple and hoping the other person will get sick or die.

Questions to think about:

1. Which of these excuses have you used?

2. What is your justifications for each excuse?

3. Work on your memory verses, Proverbs 3:13-22.

How …
And the …
For her …
And her …
She is …
And nothing …
Long life…
In her…
Her ways …
And all …
She is …
And all …
The Lord …
By understanding …
By His …
And the …
My son, _____ them not _____ from your _____;
Keep _____ _____ and _____,
So they will be _____ to _____ _____
And _____ to _____ _____.

Week 5 / Day 5

What Forgiveness Means

When a man's ways are pleasing to the Lord,
He makes even his enemies to be at peace with him.

Proverbs 16:7

God is on His throne, and He can change the hearts of men. Your responsibility is to live with integrity before the Lord; He will provide for you and protect you. It all goes back to trusting in the Lord and what He tells you in His Word. Look at some misunderstandings which people have about forgiveness.

Forgiveness does not mean:

1. Letting go of healthy forms of anger.
2. Allowing others to continue to disrespect your needs and boundaries.
3. Lying down and becoming a human doormat.
4. Telling the wrongdoer that the past is no longer significant and everything's fine now.
5. Agreeing to become best buddies with the wrongdoer.
6. Pretending to go back to normal relations as if nothing happened.
7. Denying that you may still have to live with pain caused by the wrongful deed.[23]

Forgiveness does mean:

1. You will let go of the demand for repayment, particularly as you have exhausted all reasonable attempts at restitution or restoration.
2. You will free yourself to focus on rewarding relationships and pursuits.
3. You will choose to give up any obsessions regarding the wrongdoer, recognizing, instead, that you have better things to give your attention to.
4. You will be willing to refrain from the ongoing temptation to insult the wrongdoer.
5. You will let go of any illusions that you might somehow control the wrongdoer's life.
6. You will be forward-looking about life, realizing that new opportunities await you.
7. You will give yourself permission to make life choices that will lead to contentment and peace.[24]

Part of my forgiveness journey was the fear of having to stay in a relationship with the person who hurt me. When I realized forgiveness did not mean I would have to put myself back into an unhealthy relationship, I was able to take another step towards trusting God. Boundaries are necessary in any relationship. The Bible never says to forgive and forget. God forgives and forgets your transgressions and throws them as far as the east is from the west, but you are not asked to do so. It is healthy to remember past abuses, learn from them, and not put yourself in a relationship that will repeat them. A battered wife who divorces her husband and marries another wife-beater hasn't remembered. A sexually abused child who abuses another or gets into a relationship with another abuser, doesn't remember. You should remember so you can put healthy boundaries on your present relationships. When I forgave, trusted God, and put healthy boundaries on the relationship with the one who hurt me, I was able to realize I might never be able to have a relationship with him. I am okay with this, but I continually pray for a change in his heart.

Two wonderful books on boundaries are: *Boundaries: When to Say Yes When to Say No to Take Control of Your Life* by Henry Cloud and John Townsend[25], and *Boundaries: Where You End and I Begin* by Anne Katherine.[26]

Remember Philippians 3:13-14 said you are to put the past behind and reach forward? Well, that is what forgiveness allows you to do: to look to the future with expectation and joy!

Letting Go

To let go doesn't mean to stop caring,
it means I can't do it for someone else.
To let go is not to cut myself off,
it's the realization that I can't control another.
To let go is not to enable,
but to allow learning from natural consequences.
To let go is to admit powerlessness,
which means the outcome is not in my hands.
To let go is not to try to change or blame another,
I can only change myself.
To let go is not to care for,
but to care about.
To let go is not to fix,
but to be supportive.
To let go is not to judge,
but to allow another to be a human being.
To let go is not to be in the middle arranging all the outcomes,
but to allow others to affect their own outcomes.
To let go is not to be protective,
but to permit another to face reality.
To let go is not to deny,
but to accept.
To let go is not to nag, scold, or argue,

but to search out my own shortcomings and to correct them.
To let go is not to adjust everything to my desires,
but to take each day as it comes.
To let go is not to criticize and regulate anyone,
but to try to become what I dream I can be.
To let go is not to regret the past,
but to grow and love for the future.
To let go is to fear less and love more.[27]

Is there anyone you need to forgive right now for big things or little things? Take a few minutes and lay this situation before God choosing to forgive rather than demanding you be repaid.

Questions to think about:

1. What inaccurate meanings of forgiveness did you hold as true?

2. Are you going to choose to forgive?

3. How are you enforcing healthy boundaries in a trying relationship?

4. You should have Proverbs 3:13-22 memorized.

> How ...
> And the ...
> For her ...
> And her ...
> She is ...
> And nothing ...
> Long life ...
> In her ...
> Her ways ...
> And all ...
> She is ...
> And all ...
> The Lord ...
> By understanding ...
> By His ...
> And the ...
> My son ...
> Keep sound ...
> So they ...
> And adornment ...

Week 5 Group Discussion

1. What is your anger level?

2. Do you tend to confront the things which make you angry or do you tend to repress your anger and hurt?

3. What are some constructive suggestions you think you could employ when you are angry?

4. Practice some pretend situations which would make you angry, and role play aggressive behavior and assertive behavior.

5. How do you grieve the hurts of your life?

6. How full or empty is your emotional bucket?

7. What should pull your train–your emotions or God's Word? (Col. 3:16, James 1:21)

8. Which of the excuses in lesson four have you used?

9. What inaccurate meanings of forgiveness did you hold as true?

10. How are you enforcing healthy boundaries in a trying relationship?

11. Recite Proverbs 3:13-22 together

Week 6 / Day 1

Your Body and Food

*I urge you, brethren, by the mercies of God, to
present your bodies a living and holy sacrifice,
acceptable to God, which is your spiritual service
of worship.*

Romans 12:1

You read in the introduction to this book that God tells you, "Whatever you do in word or deed, do all in the name of the Lord Jesus." (Colossians 3:16). This includes how you treat your body. Let's see what the New Testament says about your body and how it should be treated.

Turn to 1 Corinthians 3:16. This verse will give you a foundation for this study. "Do you not know that you are a _____ _____ _____, and that the Spirit of God dwells in you?"

The Jewish temple was literally God's dwelling place. He tabernacled there upon the Ark of the Covenant on the mercy seat. The temple was the center of Jewish culture and worship. This picture is repeated in 1 Corinthians 6:19-20. "Or do you not know that your body is a _____ _____ _____ _____ _____ who is in you, whom you have from God, and that you are not your own? For you have been bought with a price; therefore, glorify God in your body."

Think about these two verses for just a minute. According to 1 Corinthians 6:20, why should you glorify God with your body? _____

What was this price? _____

The blood of Jesus paid for your sins. You are now no longer to be a slave to sin, but to righteousness. And who is your righteousness? _____

First came the transaction, then the obedience.

List ways you can glorify God in your body. Include do's and don'ts.

_____

_____

_____

_____

Hopefully your list included eating right, exercising, getting enough sleep, getting sunshine, not drinking alcohol, not doing drugs, not being a glutton, not having sex outside of marriage, etc. Are you going to obey? Turn to Proverbs to find out how to treat your body correctly. Start with your eating habits.

Do you live to eat, or eat to live?

Think about this for a minute and fill in the blanks: I _____ to _____.

Proverbs 25:16 warns you about overeating. "Have you found honey? Eat only what you _____, that you not have it in excess and vomit it." Honey is a nutritious food. It actually has healing properties within it. It is sweet and helps other foods to taste good. But even this food which is good for you can be eaten to excess and make you vomit. A good rule for food is: everything in moderation.

1 Corinthians 6:12 is a great verse to memorize. Keep in mind as you read it that you are no longer under the law, but you have freedom under grace.
According to this verse, what is lawful? _____
Are these things profitable? _____

The writer declares he will not be mastered by anything. Are you mastered by your cravings and addictions to food? When you are anxious or angry or happy do you turn to food? Do you eat what is healthy to be a good steward of your body, or do you eat what you want when you want it and allow it to be your master? There are varying degrees of misuse of food. For some it is an addiction to food, for others it might be cravings for sugary foods. You must ask yourself if this food at this moment is profitable for your body. There are a lot of nutrition books on the market. Read a few. Learn about healthy eating habits. Decide now what you are going to eat and serve to your family. Healthy children and husbands eat healthy foods.

A few rules our family has adopted about food are:
>   No white flour
>   No white sugar
>   No white rice
>   No pork

Most nutritionists agree on these four foods. We also watch for and exclude chemicals in our diet such as MSG and nitrites and nitrates. There are healthy substitutes out there. We try to eat living food (fruits, vegetables, nuts, and whole grains) at each meal and have learned to reach for the raw veggies and fruit instead of the potato chips.

This does not mean we don't occasionally celebrate with ice cream and cake for birthdays or have an occasional cookie, but we try to make at least 90% of our food choices healthy. The best way to start a healthy diet is to choose one or two things to eliminate or include. Don't try to live on celery and carrots which don't have enough nutrition by themselves.

Read a couple more Proverbs about honey and see what truths you can gain.
Proverbs 16:24 states, "Pleasant words are a honeycomb, Sweet to the soul and _____ to the bones."

In Proverbs 25:27-28, what is a man who has no control over his spirit compared to? _____
_____

Proverbs 27:7 "A sated man (stomach is full and overflowing) loathes honey (that which is desirable and sweet and nutritious), but to a famished man any bitter thing is sweet." Rewrite this Proverb in your own words:_____
_____
_____

Remember, food is a gift from God to keep you healthy and to give you energy; it is not to be your god, nor is it to be abused and keep you from a full and victorious life.

Questions to think about:

1. The temple in Jerusalem was an exquisite structure. It was overlaid in gold. How important was this building to the Jewish worshipper?

2. Is your body an exquisite dwelling place for the Lord? Why or why not.

3. What could you do to make your body a worthy dwelling place for the Holy Spirit?

Add two more verses to your memorized passage in Appendix A—verses 23-24. Underline or highlight key words. You might also want to draw pictures or make up actions.

Week 6 / Day 2

Drugs and Alcohol

Wine is a mocker, strong drink a brawler,
And whoever is intoxicated by it is not wise.

Proverbs 20:1

God's Word is pretty plain about getting drunk or intoxicated. The same rules apply to smoking and illegal drugs. It's foolish. You have probably heard about the bad effects alcohol has on a body. It kills brain cells; it is a depressant; it is addictive, etc. Let's see what else God's Word says.

Read Proverbs 23:20-21. This Proverb goes one step farther and says you should not even be with or associate with heavy drinkers or gluttons. Their fate will become yours. What is their fate according to these verses? _____
_____

Check out James 4:4 and 1 Corinthians 15:33. Summarize what these verses are teaching you. _____
_____
_____

Proverbs 23:29-35 describes the life of an alcoholic pretty well. What is wine compared to in verse 32?
_____

What are the results of too much wine? There are 10 listed.

    1.   6.

    2.   7.

    3.   8.

    4.   9.

    5.   10.

Lastly, look at Proverbs 31:1-7. Who should never drink wine according to these verses? _____
_____

Who should drink wine? _____

These are strong verses. If you want to rule and have authority over yourself, your family, your employees, your kingdom, then don't drink wine, for it will affect your decisions and judgments. If you are perishing and bitter, then go ahead and use alcohol to help you forget. Notice it will help you forget, but it does nothing to turn things around or bring you to peace.

Many Christians will point to Ephesians 5:18 and believe that a little wine is okay as long as they don't get drunk. I would like to point out though that you are to be filled with the Spirit. When you are filled with the Spirit of God there is no need for wine or strong drink. We taught our boys that if you don't want to get swept away by a roaring, turbulent river don't put even a toe in. The first step can be fatal. If your doctor orders wine for medicinal purposes, this is another matter altogether.

Bill Gothard, a Christian speaker, used to say, "What the parents do in moderation, the children will do in excess."[28] The fact that my husband and I want to be filled with the Spirit of God, and we don't want to ever give our children a negative role model has kept us to our pledge of no alcohol. If you never take the first step, you will never follow down the wide road which leads to destruction.

James 4:7-8 says to "Submit therefore to God. _____ the devil and he will flee from you. _____ near to God and He will draw near to you." You can't be in the presence of God and Satan at the same time.

Don't be where people are drinking, don't try to fit in with the crowd who drinks, and don't believe it can't happen to you, and you can handle just one drink. Most alcoholics used to believe the same thing. If you have sorrows to drown, take them to Jesus. If you have anger to work out, take it to Jesus. If you are depressed or down, take it to Jesus. He will comfort you and give you hope. Alcohol can't do that! If you need to celebrate, then dance and sing and shout joyful thanksgivings to God. Why take something that will depress you when you want to rejoice? Illegal drugs fall in this same category multiplied by ten! Any substance you rely on to try to fill the emptiness inside of you will only lead to death and destruction. Only filling up with Jesus will bring life and joy.

If you have gotten drunk before, take it to Jesus. He will forgive you and give you strength not to drink again. He may take away that desire immediately, or He may want you to cry to Him when that desire overwhelms you. Either way He promises He has provided a way out of all temptations. There are people who can help you overcome this addiction. Celebrate Recovery programs are set up in churches all over the country, and they are excellent. Don't let pride keep you from getting help.

Read 1 Corinthians 10:13. "God is _____ who will not allow you to be tempted beyond what you are able, but with the temptation will provide a way of _____ also, so that you will be able to endure it."

That's a promise! It is also a choice. For some it has to be a minute by minute choice because they have already fallen under the curse of alcohol. Choose now never to go down that path and be free from the torment and guilt that addiction brings. Cling to Jesus. He is enough!

Questions to think about:

1. Are you in a position of authority? Do you wish to be in authority some day?

2. Those in authority shouldn't drink alcohol or do drugs. Why do you think this is?

3. Explain the quote, "What the parents do in moderation, the children will do in excess."

4. Give some positive and negative examples of this.

5. Work on memorizing Proverbs 3:13-24.

> How …
> For her …
> She is …
> Long life …
> Her ways …
> She is …
> The Lord …
> By His …
> My son …
> Keep sound …
> So they …
> And adornment …
> Then you will _____ in your way securely
> And your foot will not _____.
> When you lie down, you will not _____ _____;
> When you lie down, your sleep will be _____.

Honoring Your Parents

Listen to your father who begot you,
And do not despise your mother when she is old.
The father of the righteous will greatly rejoice
And he who sires a wise son will be glad in him.
Let your father and your mother be glad,
And let her rejoice who gave birth to you.

Proverbs 23:22, 24-25

Your parents are not perfect. They are human beings just like you. They have dreams and aspirations, frustrations and failings, and good days and bad days just like you. Some parents are Christians and try to raise their children up in the fear and admonition of the Lord. Others have not come to the saving knowledge of Jesus Christ and try to raise their kids up the best they can in human understanding. Still others are distracted, uncaring, and abusive. Either way, they are human and they will make mistakes and let you down.

As infants and small children, we all think our parents are perfect. We want to be just like them. They are our first role models. Then as we grow and mature, we begin to realize they aren't perfect, and sometimes, we don't want to be just like them. What does the Bible say about how we should respond to our parents—whether they be good or bad parents? As we study these verses you will begin to realize God does not put parents into separate groups of good and bad, but rather, He expects you to honor them no matter what. This can be difficult.

How can a son or daughter honor an alcoholic dad or an abusive mom? Notice in the verse above Solomon mentions the mother who gave birth to you. At the very least you should be thankful to your parents for giving you life. Your mom went through an awful lot of pain to bring you into this world. For that you should honor her.

Most of us have parents who, at least, fed us regularly and gave us a bed and clothes to wear. For that be thankful and honor your parents.

Proverbs 20:20 says, "He who _____ his father or his mother, His lamp (eye) will go out in time of darkness."

If you have nothing positive to say about your parents, don't say anything at all. You honor your parents by not speaking badly of them. This is hard to do, especially if they have a critical spirit or a bitter tongue. However, you are accountable to a holy God who has given you His command to "Honor your father and mother." (Matt. 19:19).

In Exodus 20:12 God tells the Israelites to, "_____ your father and your mother, that your days may be prolonged in the land which the Lord your God gives you."

He restates this to His children of grace in Ephesians 6:1 when He says, "Children, obey your parents in the Lord, for this is right." He then quotes the verses from Exodus. So, if you are single and still in their home, obeying your parents is a way of honoring them. You should obey them not just in action, but in attitude. God will bless your response. If you are out on your own or married, you do not have to obey your parents because you are no longer a child. However, you are to continue to honor them.

If they expect obedience, you need to set clear and definite boundaries letting them know you are an adult and no longer required to obey them. If they choose to respect you, then they can discuss their desires and give you advice knowing that you have a right to refuse.

Will your parents make you mad? Probably. Should they always give in when you want something? Probably not. This adult relationship goes both ways. If you no longer have to obey them, you still need to respect them. Try to establish an adult to adult relationship. If this is not possible, then put boundaries on the relationship that honors them and keeps you safe and independent. Are your parents always right? Probably not, but they love you. They were given a mandate from God to raise you up. If you can't trust your parents, then trust your God.

From the text above, what two things can you do to honor your parents?
   1.
   2.

Look up each of these verses from Proverbs and fill in the blanks. Ladies, remember God is speaking to and about you, also.

Proverbs 10:1 "A wise son makes a father _____, but a foolish son is a _____ to his mother."

Proverbs 13:1 "A wise son _____ his father's discipline, but a scoffer does not listen to rebuke."

Proverbs 16:31 "A grey head is a crown of _____, It is found in the way of righteousness." (Even though your parents may not be up on the newest technology, or the newest use of the English language, they have had many more experiences and have gained knowledge and wisdom.)

Proverbs 23:15-16 "My son, if your heart is _____, my own heart also will be

_____; and my inmost being will rejoice when your lips speak what is right."

Proverbs 27:11 "Be wise, my son, and make my heart _____, that I may reply to him who reproaches me."

Proverbs 29:3 "A man who loves _____ makes his father glad, but he who keeps company with harlots wastes his wealth." (Remember in the Old Testament, harlotry was a symbol for all sin, idolatry in particular.)

According to these verses, how can a son or daughter (even as an adult) make their parents glad? _____
_____
_____
_____

I had wanted to attend a Christian college. My parents wanted me to attend the junior college in our town because the coach for the Pan Am softball team coached there. I got a full ride scholarship. I could have kicked and cried about not attending the college of my choice. I made a conscience effort to honor my parents and went to the junior college. After the first semester, I had torn my shoulder and could no longer pitch. I moved to Texas where my parents had relocated. They allowed me to attend the Christian university in their small Texas town. Here I met my husband. Honoring has served me well.

Questions to think about:

1. If your parents are alive, ask them if they feel like you honor them. Write their response here.

2. If they have died, how can you honor them?

3. If you can't respect your parents because of their lifestyle choices, how can you still honor them? (You may not respect the president in the white house at any given time, but you can honor the position which he fills.)

4. List some things that you are grateful for about your parents.

5. Keep memorizing Proverbs 3:13-24.

    How …
    For her …
    She is …
    Long life …
    Her ways …
    She is…
    The Lord…
    By His …

My son …
Keep sound …
So they …
And adornment …
Then you will _____ in your way _____
And your _____ will not _____.
When you _____ _____, you will not _____ _____;
When you _____ _____, your sleep will be _____.

Your Heavenly Father

He who assaults his father and drives his mother away,
Is a shameful and disgraceful son.

Proverbs 19:26

Parents—you can't live with them and you can't live without them! Yesterday you looked at some verses which told you how to treat your parents.

1. Do not speak badly of them.
2. Honor them.

Today you will look at what not to do in order to honor them. The verse above says you should not assault your father or drive your mother away. This would include verbal assault and physical assault. God is very serious about this. In the Old Testament the penalty for striking your father or mother was death (Exodus 21:15). Why was God so adamant about this? Parents are God's representatives on earth for Himself. He is your heavenly Father. We all tend to relate to God as we relate to our earthly fathers. (We'll talk more about this in just a minute.) God demands and requires you to honor Him, so He must insist you honor your earthly parents as His representatives.

Describe your father: _____

_____

_____

_____

If you have never known your father, or he is no longer a part of your life write *absent*.

Your father is human. If he is a loving, caring, gentle man, then you probably are able to accept God's love and gentleness. If your father is harsh, or judgmental, or only gives love with conditions, then you probably see God as demanding and judgmental. This is why it is so important to read the Word of God and get an accurate picture of your Heavenly Father. It may take someone years to be able to transfer the truths about God as Father from their head to their heart because of the misrepresentation of Him through their earthly father. But when they get to know the true character of God, they can have a Heavenly Father of whom they are no longer afraid. They will be able to climb into His lap, sit at His feet, twirl in joy before Him, and repent, knowing He will forgive with compassion, and they can bother Him daily with their requests because He cares.

Search through Scripture to find the true nature of your Father. His character can be found in the Old and New Testaments. I keep a notebook by my Bible and have an ongoing list of His attributes. A good place to start is in the Psalms.

I love the picture which Psalm 37:23-24 presents.
> The steps of a man are established by the Lord,
> And He _____ in his way.
> When he falls, he will not be hurled headlong,
> Because the _____ is the One
> who _____ _____ _____.

What a great picture! Do you see it? Think of a father teaching his child to walk. The father is holding the hand of the little one. The father is taking great joy in his little boy or girl. Suddenly the child topples and falls. The father does not scold or get angry. No, I see him laughing and getting down on his knees and picking up the child, comforting him/her, setting her back on his/her feet and taking delight in the entire process!

I think this is how God relates to your failures. To Him it is just a topple, a fall. He claps at you for trying, sets you back on your feet, holds your hand, and points you in the direction He has already established for you. God delights in you! Take a minute and let this sink in. It doesn't matter what you have done, what you think you are, or even if you are involved in something right now you need to repent of. God delights in you just because you are His child. He created you, loves you, and takes joy in you!

Matthew 6 contains the words, "Our Father who is in heaven." The Lord's Prayer follows. Actually it is an example prayer of what you can say and ask of God. Verse 8 even reminds you, "Your Father knows what you need before you ask Him."

You can't remember being an infant. But think about how an infant is taken care of. He can't speak or explain what his needs are, but the parent knows. When it is time to eat, he is fed. When it is time to sleep, he is rocked to sleep. When he needs to be cleaned, the diaper is changed. A cry may come to get the parent's attention, but the parent knows and is just waiting to be summoned. So it is with God. He knows your needs for love, affection, affirmation, healing, forgiveness, self-acceptance, food, clothing, etc. before you even ask. He is just waiting for you to summon Him. And He is delighted when you do.

How does this fit in with not assaulting your earthly parents? They are God's representatives. If you assault them, you have, in essence, dishonored Him. If you don't respect your mom and dad, then at least, treat them as God's representatives and don't curse them or assault them. Even better, forgive them. This one can be tough! But God's grace and love and forgiveness can lead someone to forgive a mom or dad who was never there, a parent who was abusive, a parent who belittled and angered their child, a mom who didn't teach her daughter about womanhood, or a dad who didn't teach his son about being a man or who didn't represent godliness.

Remember no one has perfect parents. You need to forgive your parents for their mistakes and shortcomings. Take responsibility for your own life and move on. Talk to God; ask Him to put His kind of forgiveness into your heart. What release! What freedom! What joy! Then you can accept a Heavenly Father's love and be His little boy or girl.

Proverbs 30:17 gives you another admonition. "The eye that _____ a father and _____ a mother, the ravens of the valley will pick it out and the young eagles will eat it." Gruesome, but effective!

Proverbs 28:24 says: "He who _____ his father or his mother and says, 'It is not a transgression,' is the companion of a man who destroys."

This verse would indicate robbing them of their material goods, but you must be careful also not to rob them of their dignity, their hope, and their joy.

Be careful of your words and attitudes towards your parents. As they age, they will become more dependent. Give compassion and grace by being patient, caring, and loving.

Two excellent books for understanding your relationship with your parents better are Dr. Robert McGee's book *Search for Significance: Seeing Your True Worth Through God's Eyes*[29] and McGee's and Craddock's book, *The Parent Factor.*[30]

Questions to think about:

1. How important is it to God that you honor you parents?

2. If someone does not honor their parents, they are worthy of death according to Romans 1:28-32. Why do you think this is?

3. How can you honor your parents?

4. List some characteristics of your Heavenly Father.

5. Work on your memory verses, Proverbs 3:13-24.

> How …
> For her …
> She is …
> Long life …
> Her ways …
> She is …

The Lord ...
By His ...
My son ...
Keep sound ...
So they ...
And adornment ...
Then you will _____ in _____ _____ _____
And your _____ will _____ _____.
When you _____ _____, you will _____ _____ _____;
When you _____ _____, your _____ will be _____.

Raising Children

Train up a child in the way he should go,
Even when he is old he will not depart from it.

Proverbs 22:6

You may be fortunate to be raising children or helping with grandchildren. Even if you don't have children, this lesson can help you when you come into contact with children.

Many sermons have been preached on Proverbs 22:6. Look at what this verse doesn't mean and what it does. First of all, this verse does not mean if you pound Bible verses into a child's head, he will never sin! This verse does not mean if you decide a child should be a doctor and train him in medicine, he will be a doctor. This also does not mean if you train a child in righteousness, pray for them daily, take them to church, etc., they won't go their own way for a time.

Remember salvation is an individual choice. Your grown children have a free will of their own. If you have a child who grows up and goes the way of the world, don't blame yourself. Satan can sure get a foothold on your life with false guilt. Instead, love them, pray for them, and give them grace to be able to return without enabling them. If you raise a child in God's Word and pray for them daily, it is very likely, eventually, they will return to the teaching of their childhood and become a Christian living a righteous life.

What this verse does mean is each child has a natural bent, a God given personality. If you, as the parent, train them up in the way in which they personally should go within their personality and with wisdom from God's Word, then they will not depart from it. If your child is compassionate and caring, artistic and creative then don't insist they take technical drafting. Rather, let them explore the arts or the healing crafts. If your child builds cathedrals with his blocks which are ornate and technical, you might encourage him to be an engineer or lawyer. Explore the different careers with him/her which are available within his/her interests. Don't belittle or degrade a child for what, by nature, he/she enjoys. Be sure to let boys be boys and girls be girls. God did create them uniquely different. Help them to celebrate this difference and revel in who God made them to be!

Some children are readers, others are doers. Each child has a learning style, how they interpret their world. Are they visual, audio, kinesthetic, or oral learners? My visual learner was an early reader. My kinesthetic learner could learn anything if he did a project with it. My audio learner did great in college where he showed up for classes and listened to the lectures. An oral learner may need to talk out loud to process the information he is learning. There are a lot of books on learning styles. (*The Way They Learn* by Cynthia Tobias[31] and *The Big What Now Book of Learning Styles* by Carol Barnier[32] are both great books to get you started.) Learn to know your child. You can figure out their learning style by taking them for a walk. When you get home, say, "Tell me about your walk." The visual child will tell you what he saw. The kinesthetic child will tell you what he did. The audio child will tell you what he heard. The oral child will tell you every detail over and over!

Some children have different learning weaknesses as well. My dyslexic children really had a hard time spelling. We worked on spelling and introduced typing and spell check early! My ADHD child needed rigid structure for safety and to process. My visual learner needed a lot more assignments, or I would find him hiding a reading book behind his math book! Learn your child. Some are right brained and some left or whole brained. Right brained children tend to be artistic and random; left brain children tend to be technical and literal. One makes great interior designers and the other will do well in accounting. *Right Brained Kids in a Left Brained World* by Jeffrey Freed[33] is an excellent book for any parent. There is so much out there on biblical parenting–become an expert about your child.

The Five Love Languages of Children by Gary Chapman[34] taught me how to approach my children with love and with discipline. My oldest child's love language is service. When he was at home, I would sneak into his room while he was taking a shower and make his bed. He thought I was the best mom ever! Another child had the love language of touch. If I rubbed his back or put a hand on his shoulder, he felt loved and appreciated. Another son responded to gifts. The love languages are: touch, gifts, time, words of affirmation, and service. Your child has one or a combination of these love languages. Watch how he/she shows love to others and this will give you a big hint!

My experience as a mom, a Sunday School teacher, a staff wife at various churches, and a friend is that choosing to put young children in a school setting for eight hours a day and then taking them to church for only two hours on a Sunday is not sufficient training to raise godly children. You must train your kids not only in their bent and according to their learning styles, but you must train them in righteousness. This takes consistency and hard work. A family devotional and prayer time in the morning, personal Bible readings, and a biblical lesson at night as well as in the course of each day is the minimal it will take to ground your children in God's Word. Don't assume the church, the youth group, the Christian school, etc. is doing your job for you. These precious little ones are your responsibility as a parent and nothing can replace you. You can get some creative for teaching your children the Bible with my book, *As They Sit and Stand: A Resource and Guide for Teaching Your Children the Bible.*[35]

Read Deuteronomy 6:7. When should you teach your children about God? _____
_____
_____

Your goal as a parent is not to raise perfect children but godly children. They are in process and that's okay. You are too. Children raised to be perfect will always feel dissatisfied with themselves. Perfect children raised by the law and no grace become demanding, perfectionistic, rebellious, depressed, and angry. Children raised to be godly, upholding the law but with a measure of grace, will become children of faith, freedom, and fulfillment.

Parenting requires consistency and diligence. Children respond best when there are clear cut expectations, rules, routines, and consequences. Have a plan and follow it through. Remember they are watching you. They will do what you do rather than what you say.

Proverbs 29:15 says, "The rod and reproof give wisdom, but a child who gets his _____ _____ brings shame to his mother."

Remember being an example is a much better teacher than just telling your kids what to do. Your number one directive is to enjoy these unique little people.

Questions to think about:

If you have children or grandchildren answer the following questions. If you do not have children in your daily life, think about yourself as you answer these questions.

1. What are some of your children's natural bents?

2. What are their learning styles?

3. Do they have learning difficulties? How can you compensate for these?

4. Perfect your memory verses, Proverbs 3:13-24.

> How …
> For her …
> She is …
> Long life …
> Her ways …
> She is …
> The Lord …
> By His …
> My son …
> Keep sound …
> So they …
> And adornment…
> Then you …
> And your…
> When you …
> When you …

Week 6 Group Discussion

1. The temple in Jerusalem was an exquisite structure. It was overlaid in gold. How important was this building to the Jewish worshipper? (1 Kings 8:10-1)

2. Is your body an exquisite dwelling place for the Lord? What could you do to make your body a worthy dwelling place for the Holy Spirit?

3. Those in authority don't drink alcohol or do drugs. Why do you think this is?

4. Explain the quote, "What the parents do in moderation, the children will do in excess."

5. Give some positive and negative examples of this.

6. If you can't respect your parents because of their lifestyle choices, how can you still honor them?

7. List some things you are grateful for about your parents.

8. Why is it important to God that you honor our parents?

9. List some characteristics of your Heavenly Father. (Ps. 103:8-14)

10. Recite Proverbs 3:13-24 together.

Love and Marriage

Better is a dish of vegetables where love is,
Than a fattened ox served with hatred.

Proverbs 15:17

I am married to the most compassionate, loving, interesting, fun-loving husband ever. I used to be married to a hypercritical, angry, uninteresting man. I did not divorce or kill my first husband, but I did learn a really important lesson–If you don't like who you are married to, change your responses and your tactics! I became content, interested, fun, and engaged, and voila! So did the man of my dreams!

Comedian Rita Rudner claims, "I love being married! It's so great to have found one special person that I get to annoy for the rest of my life!"[36]

Martin Luther spoke on marriage as well saying, "There is no more lovely, friendly, or charming relationship, communion, or company than that of a good marriage"[37]

Marriage matters to God, you and your spouse, your children, the church, the culture, and to Satan and his demons. Civilizations fall when marriages fail. And Christian marriages are on the front lines.

Marriage matters to God. God uses marriage as an illustration of His covenant relationship with first Israel and then the church. In Isaiah 50:1 and Jeremiah 3:8 you see God gave a writ of divorce to Israel. He promises to call His bride, the church, home for the marriage feast. He is the Bridegroom. As part of the church, you are the bride. Through this union, God teaches you about His relationship to you. This is your hope and your reality as you relate to Jesus now and in eternity. It's a journey towards intimacy with your Creator.

Jesus desires to be your husband (partner). To delight in you, to protect you, to provide for you. He desires to have an emotionally intimate relationship with you through prayer. As the earthly temple of the Israelites was a form or copy of the real temple in heaven, so also your earthly marriage is a form or copy of the heavenly marriage to come. In Israel a young woman waits expectantly and joyfully for her soon-to-be husband to come and collect her and her maidens and lead them to the marriage ceremony and feast. Are you waiting in anticipation for Jesus to come and take you to the marriage celebration where you will be joined with Him for eternity?

Marriage matters to our culture. Several times Moses prayed for God to hold back His divine wrath from the Israelites when they sinned against God. Moses' reasoning was that other nations were watching and they needed to see God bring His children into the Promised Land victoriously. The same is true of today's Christian marriages. The world needs to see us work at our marriages, strive for greater love in our homes, and come out victoriously. This doesn't mean perfection or never facing troubles, but it does mean in the midst of life's circumstances husband and wife pull together and with God's guidance they make it through stronger, more determined, with a sweeter and more enduring love, and ready to help others.

Marriage matters to the spouses. Married people are healthier, happier, and tend to live longer. Security, acceptance, unconditional love, loyalty, sympathy, encouragement, partnership are all benefits of a loving marriage.

When we first married my husband gave me a plaque that read:

> I once thought marriage took
> Just two to make a go,
> But now I am convinced
> It takes the Lord also.
>
> And not one marriage fails
> Where Christ is asked to enter,
> As lovers come together
> With Jesus at the center.
>
> But marriage seldom thrives,
> And homes are incomplete,
> Till He is welcomed there
> To help avoid defeat.
>
> In homes where Christ is first,
> It's obvious to see,
> Those unions really work,
> For marriage still takes three.[38]

Think of marriage as a triangle. God is the apex and the wife and husband are the two lower angles. If you put your fingers on the lower corners and slide them towards the apex, you will see your fingers come closer together as get the closer to the top. When both the husband and wife are pursuing a closer relationship to God, they will find themselves closer together.

This is why it is so important not to be unequally yoked to an unbeliever. In her book *The Confident Woman: Know*

Who You Are in Christ, Anabel Gillham puts it this way, "When my spirit is pervaded with the Spirit of Jesus and when my husband's spirit is pervaded with the Spirit of Jesus, we then become 'one spirit with Him' (1 Cor. 6:17). Our goals, our desires, and our attitudes will be the same, but because we are different in the other areas (physically, emotionally, and perceptually), there will always be two different approaches to those goals; there will be two different needs, two different emotions, two different perceptions. And yet understanding and mutual give-and-take will be possible because of our oneness of spirit."[39]

She continues, "The spiritual "attitude" is the essence of spiritual oneness. It is agape love, unconditional love, and it is already ours because of our identity in Christ: giving, self-denial, servitude, and humility all practiced willingly, motivated by love."[40]

Realize love will not hold your marriage together, but your marriage will hold your love together. This is why living together does not work. The commitment to each other and to God's ways will be the glue that sticks and holds.

Read Proverbs 12:4. "An excellent wife is the _____ of her husband, but she who _____ him is like rottenness in his bones.

Proverbs 18:22 says, "He who finds a wife finds a good thing and obtains _____ from the Lord.

Proverbs 19:14 claims, "House and wealth are an inheritance from fathers, but a _____ wife is from the _____."

What does it mean to be prudent? _____

In Proverbs 5:18 an attitude and the results are found. "Let your fountain be _____, and _____ in the wife of your youth." Women, substitute the word *husband* for *wife*.

Marriage matters to children. God hates divorce. Divorce will devastate your children. Dr. James Dobson says the relationship which is most important to a child is not the relationship between the child and the mother or the child and the father, but rather the relationship between the mother and the father. When this relationship is stable, then the child feels safe and secure and is free to grow and learn and make mistakes and be disciplined and still know he/she is okay. If you have been divorced know God's grace covers you and you are free to move forward in a relationship of grace with Him. Be aware of your children's confusion, anger, and need for affirmation. Keep the communication lines open.

Think of the marriage as the hub of a wheel, God is the axle, and the spokes are your children, and activities–even ministry. From that solid piece of wood, the hub, the spokes go out and reach the circle wheel itself. When that hub is solid and tied into the axle firmly, a spoke can break and even though the wheel may be off kilter, the rest of the spokes can hold it together for a time. But if the hub breaks, the whole wheel goes flying off the axle and is no longer a viable unit. All the pieces are useless unless that hub is sturdy. If your marriage is not stable, your children's emotional and spiritual health are in peril as well as those of yourself and your husband.

Marriage matters so very much, I would challenge you that if your marriage is in trouble, you may need to put aside some other pursuits for a time or lower your expectations, and get the marriage healthy because then, and only then, can you be successful in life. Seek help from a Christian counselor, pastor, or older woman in the church. There is no shame in asking for guidance to better yourself and your marriage. You must not just be on the defense about your marriage; you must go on the offense.

A quick word on abuse: abuse is when one person does not allow the other to have their own thoughts, opinions, or feelings. It may include physical abuse as well as emotional and mental abuse. As a daughter of the King, you do not deserve abuse. If you are in an abusive situation, please seek help.

Living Beautifully: Practical Proverbs for Women Book 1[41] covers the role of sex in a marriage and the caution of keeping the marriage bed undefiled (before and during the marriage). Here are a few verses to reiterate this point.

Proverbs 6:29: "So is the one who goes in to his neighbor's wife; Whoever touches her will not _____ _____.

Read Proverbs 5:2-14. What are the results of adultery? _____
_____
_____
_____

Questions to think about:

1. Are you a prudent wife? (If you are single, are you a prudent woman?)

2. Why is it important to your marriage to keep growing closer to God?

3. Why does Christian marriage matter to our culture and its view of God?

You will finish up the memorization of Proverbs 3:13-26 this week. Turn to Appendix A and underline or highlight any key words. You might also want to draw or act out these verses.

Characteristics of Godly Men and Women

Like a bird that wanders from her nest,
So is a man who wanders from his home.

Proverbs 27:8

This is true for men and women. The home must be a priority. It is in a home you grow as a Christian and as a person. It is a safe place. The home is where love rules and children are nurtured. It is where you can get recharged, lick your wounds and recover, and are protected and secure. Not all homes are this way because of sin. If you did not grow up in a home where you were safe, you can still provide safety and security for your spouse and children with God's love and healing.

Titus 2:2-8 has a lot to teach us about the home and the relationships and priorities within our homes. Older men would include any who are spiritually mature and have taken on the responsibility of wife or wife and children.

List the characteristics given for an older man.
1.
2.
3.
4.
5.
6.

List the characteristics for an older woman.
1.
2.
3.
4.
5.

List the characteristics the older woman is to teach the younger women.

1.

2.

3.

4.

5.

6.

7.

What reason is given in Titus 2:5 for such behavior? _____

_____

Women, being a worker at home is not a popular teaching in today's world, but it is biblical. The Bible does not prohibit women from working. The Proverbs 31 wise woman bought a field and planted it for gain. She also makes and sells linen garments and belts to the tradesmen. However, her main priority was her home.

When things are going smoothly at home, all members of the family are more secure, more relaxed, and are able to focus on other things. I have found it is essential to stay at home with the children when they are young if at all possible. They need the security and training of their parents. A home of a grandparent or other loving adult could be an option if the woman must work. But home is best. There the children will grow up with a sense of belonging, feeling loved, secure, safe, and ready to venture into new situations. The home is the foundation.

We chose to continue to homeschool our children through the high school years. This is an individual choice and is between each family and God. No matter how you choose to educate your children, Deuteronomy 6:7 tells you it is your responsibility to teach God's precepts and words to your children. It requires time and relationship to teach and model a godly life for your children. This is best accomplished at home. The home must be your first tower of defense against an evil and sinful generation and culture. Careers can wait. Children cannot. They will grow up with or without God's Word and with or without parents–this will shape their lives.

List the characteristics of a young man from Titus 2:6-8.

1.

2.

3.

4.

5.

Ladies, if you are single, this is a good measure of a man for consideration.

Questions to think about:

1. What might someone have to give up to be a worker at home?

2. What might someone gain by being a worker at home?

3. If you are a young woman, what characteristics do you need to pray about for wisdom and practice?

4. If you are a seasoned woman of years, what characteristics do you need to pray about for wisdom and practice?

5. Do you know a godly man according to these lists?

6. Start memorizing Proverbs 3:13-26.

> How …
> For her …
> She is …
> Long life …
> Her ways …
> She is …
> The Lord …
> By His …
> My son …
> So they …
> Then you …
> And your …
> When you …
> When you …
> Do not be afraid of _____ fear
> Nor of the onslaught of the _____ when it comes;
> For the Lord will be your _____
> And will keep your _____ from being caught.

Characteristics of a Godly Man

*He who finds a wife finds a good thing
and obtains favor from the Lord.*

Proverbs 18:22

The men in our lives are as human as we are. They have choices to make every day. Turn to these verses and write down your thoughts on how a man should behave.

Psalm 127:1 _____

_____

Matthew 7:24 _____

_____

Ephesians 5:25, 28 _____

_____

Ephesians 5:33 _____

_____

1 Peter 3:7 _____

_____

Colossians 3:19 _____

_____

There are other verses including many which you have gone over in Proverbs about the love a man should have for his wife and the loyalty he should use to honor her.

In the book, *His Needs, Her Needs: Building an Affair-Proof Marriage*, Willard F. Harley, Jr. explains that a woman's first need is for affection. Affection includes words of affirmation, hugging, kissing, hand holding, non-sexual touching, and a wink of acknowledgement while in a crowd. Other top five needs for a woman in marriage are conversation, honesty and openness, financial commitment, and family commitment. Men's number one need is sexual fulfillment followed by recreational companionship, an attractive spouse, domestic support, and admiration.[42]

There is a cycle here. If a woman's needs are met, she will be filled up to meet husband's needs. If she meets his needs, he will be filled up to meet hers, etc. If your needs are not being met, humble yourself and give to your husband. The way to get your needs met is to meet his needs. You may also need to communicate this pattern to your spouse in order to have open honest discussion. You may have to tell him what your needs are. Men are not overly intuitive. Straight forward conversation is best. This requires humility.

Women are naturally more intuitive and have insights which lead to good decisions. Men are usually more compartmentalized and can't always see the forest because of the trees. You can help by giving your husband the bigger picture and filling in the details.

When a person takes on the responsibility of a family, it is time to grow up. It is no longer about just himself/herself. It is time to be sensible—thinking through to the consequences of actions and words; planning ahead for the financial stability of family; putting the needs of others above his own. It is time to be an example of good deeds. A man's wife and children will look to him as a godly example of leadership, servanthood, unconditional love, responsibility, and godly fun. Having come from an abusive home, my husband's unconditional love paved the way for me to truly accept God's fatherhood for myself. As he exhibited these traits and characteristics, I learned what it meant to be loved by a God who was my Heavenly Father.

Men are to be pure in doctrine, the spiritual leaders of their home. The wife should not be the one initiating prayer, taking the kids to church, teaching Bible stories, etc. This is your husband's role. And to do it well, he will need to have spent time on his own knees and in the Word so his teaching is correct and accurate. Having other godly men in his life will also help with this.

If your husband refuses to accept his God-given role, then you must step in and make sure the children are trained in the Scriptures. But never belittle your husband for not choosing to lead.
1 Peter 3:1-2 says, "In the same way, you wives, be submissive to your own husbands so that even if any of them are disobedient to the word, they may be won without a word by the behavior of their wives, as they observe your chaste and respectful behavior." Don't nag—show by example.

You are to be his greatest supporter and encourager. Bounce ideas off of each other. Discuss theological and spiritual matters. Seek to undergird his efforts. Never be critical, show contempt, or complain. Have honest discussions, but use a lot of *I* statements. ("I need you to clarify for me, I am not understanding your motivation here, etc.) Show respect through your words. Ephesians 5:33 says, "Nevertheless, each individual among you also is to _____ his own wife even as himself, and the wife must see to it that she _____ her husband."

Respectful words might include:

"I'm glad you're my husband."
"Your wisdom in such matters is incredible!"
"I am so proud of you!"
"Thank you for all your hard work to provide so well for us."

Darian Cooper's book, *You Can Be the Wife of a Happy Husband: Discovering the Keys to Marital Success*[43], isn't about changing your husband, but rather about changing your responses to him. Try being flirty and fun, supportive and encouraging. You will probably see a change in your husband's responses in return.

Cherish is the word I think of when I think about how a husband should treat his wife. You are precious, breakable, beautiful, and a princess. The husband is told to love his wife as Christ loves the church (Eph. 5:25). A man should treasure his wife's insight, her input, her personality, and her gifts. Together you can be so much more than either of you could be on your own. If you were just alike, there would not be a need for one of you!

If you are single, pray God will bring you to a point of contentment, and seek friendships with godly single men and women and/or godly couples.

Questions to think about:

1. If you are married, are you careful to support and encourage your husband?

2. Is criticism, complaining, or showing contempt is an issue you need to purge from your life?

3. What are some words of respect and appreciation you can speak to your husband?

4. Singles, what characteristics should you be seeking in a male friend?

5. Work on your memorization of Proverbs 3:13-26.

> How …
> For her …
> She is …
> Long life …
> Her ways …
> She is…
> The Lord …
> By His …
> My son …
> So they …
> Then you …
> And your …

When you …
When you …
Do not be _____ of _____ fear
Nor of the _____ of the _____ when it comes;
For the _____ will be your _____
And will keep your _____ from _____ _____.

Week 7 / Day 4

Characteristics of a Godly Woman

*As a ring of gold in a swine's snout
So is a beautiful woman who lacks discretion.*

Proverbs 11:22

I really didn't make that up! It really is in God's Word. But what does it mean? Let's compare it to a verse in Proverbs 31. Look at Proverbs 31:30. What characteristic is desired more than beauty?

_____

That's right. All the money and time you spend on being beautiful is for nothing if your heart and attitude is not right before the Lord. The Bible does not forbid the wearing of jewelry and make-up etc., but it does caution you not to be merely about your looks. Let's look up a couple more verses.

1 Timothy 2:9-10 What should come before beauty? _____
_____

1 Peter 3:4 What is precious in God's sight? _____
_____

There is nothing wrong with being attractive, wearing nice clothes, or using hair products. But those things will not draw you closer to God or to your husband. Become a woman of substance. Be someone who is valuable for their sweet and tender spirit before God. It is a true statement that in a home, the wife or mother sets the tone. Is your home beautiful, but your children are afraid to touch anything? Is cheerfulness and joy going to abound, or will everyone get up each morning hoping Mom is not in another bad mood?

As the feminine example for your children, daughters will emulate you and your sons will look to you to see what they should be looking for in a wife someday. Be a woman of the Word—gentle and caring.

I really struggled with the "gentle and quiet spirit" of 1 Peter. God gave me a voice which does not need a microphone in a gymnasium or on a ball field. My personality is that of a cheerleader. I love laughter and good

120

conversation. Growing up a Yankee gave me the ability to talk fast and get excited. If I interrupt someone it is just enthusiasm and not rudeness.

I moved to the South at 19, what a culture shock! My mind was several paragraphs ahead as I listened to the slow southern drawl of most my peers. God showed me even I can have a gentle and quiet spirit. God made some of us French horns. The thought goes in, rambles around for a while and comes out mellow and complete. Others of us are like trumpets. It's out our mouths before we have time to think, and it is usually loud and center stage! Which are you, a French horn or a trumpet? _____

Whichever you are, as long as you are playing God's song for your life and listening as He conducts, your music will be beautiful!

If God made you a quiet hand tool, then be sure you are in the Master's hand. If you are plugged in and wired like a power tool, be plugged in to the right power source–the Holy Spirit. Either tool can have a gentle and quiet heart. Some of us just like to tell others about it a little more and a little louder! Are you a power tool or a hand tool? _____

Again, whichever one you are, make sure you allow the Master Builder to guide your life. He has the blueprints!

Look for a few minutes at the verses in Titus which describe a young woman. Review the list of the seven characteristics an older woman is to teach a younger woman in Titus 2:4-5.

　　1.
　　2.
　　3.
　　4.
　　5.
　　6.
　　7.

Number one is to learn to love your husband. This is not infatuation or first year honeymoon love, but deep, unconditional, abiding love which will carry you through life's bumps and bruises. The marriage relationship needs to be your top priority next to God. Your husband should come before your career. Your children should come before your career, and, of course, your walk with God should be above all else. Don't give your husband the leftover crumbs of your day. Stay-at-home moms, take a rest when the kids are down for naps. With older children have a one hour required break for everyone other after lunch. Mom, no laundry, dishes, meals, etc. Enjoy a magazine, talk to a friend, shave your legs, etc. When your husband comes home, you will have something left to give to him.

Loving your children extends beyond caring for their physical needs. That is a part of it, but they are young and impressionable. What impression do you want to make upon them? This will take time and attention. It will take the habit of being there and leaving good memories of your consistency in your child's mind. You can do it. There is no greater joy than motherhood when the children have been raised to mind, to love, and to work.

Then surely Proverbs 10:1 can become a reality.

Write Proverbs 10:1 here. _____

_____

Titus 2 says you are to be sensible. Being sensible means to run the home with forethought and wisdom. Budgeting, nutrition, cleanliness, routine, etc. fall under this topic. Be a student of other great women who have gone before you. Learn from their books, their lives, their examples and pattern your home after godly women. Your home should exude peace and tranquility (even with toddlers about!). See the book suggestions in Appendix D.

The next characteristic is purity. This is not only in sexual areas, but also in your thought life. Be aware because what you put into your mind will mold your character. Soap operas, romance novels, etc. are not appropriate entertainment material for a Christian woman. There are a lot of movies and books which are encouraging and uplifting. Focus on these. Purity in speech includes not gossiping, not cursing, not speaking in anger, etc. A general rule is: if you don't want it overheard, don't say it! My husband and I would often retreat to the parked car in the driveway if we wanted to discuss something privately. Little ears can hear through doors.

We already spoke about being workers at home. The next trait is to be kind. Go about doing good. Speak words of kindness. Look for ways to serve others. The best way to make a friend is to be a friend. Don't forget your girlfriends once you marry. You need each other. God created women for relationships. Keep a balance between friends and husband, knowing your husband can't meet all of your social needs.

Being subject to your own husband is not being a door mat. It means you dress modestly, look to your husband for leadership, protection, and provision. It means you share your opinions and feelings respectfully. It means being the wonderful princess God created you to be, but understanding God also ordained for you to be cared for by another.

Healthy communication is essential to a healthy marriage. It is based on trust. It is important to your husband that what happens in the bedroom (or any other room of the house) stays in that room. Don't go about tale bearing. What does Proverbs 11:13 say about talebearers? _____

_____

_____

Some great principles for healthy communication include:

1. When you listen, give each other your full concentration.
2. Become truly interested in what the other is saying.
3. Hear one another out–completely and calmly
4. Make sure you understand the other's motivation and heart before you respond. It is helpful to paraphrase their conversation (I hear you saying…).
5. Emote when you respond. Emoting means to give him an emotional feedback first such as "I can tell that really upset you." Use emotion words in your response and try to enter into his state of mind.

6. Be honest but loving.
7. Be open-minded.
8. Give feedback. If you need time to process and pray, agree to finish the discussion later.

Questions to think about:

1. Is it wrong to be beautiful and to enhance your looks with make up or pretty clothes?

2. What should be your first priority in preparing yourself for marriage?

3. How can you initiate changes into your communication patterns?

4. You are almost done with memorizing Proverbs 3:13-26. Stay diligent.

How …
For her …
She is …
Long life …
Her ways …
She is …
The Lord …
By His …
My son …
So they …
Then you …
And your …
When you …
When you …
Do not be _____ of _____
Nor of the _____ of the _____ when ____ _____;
For the _____ will be _____ _____
And will _____ your _____ from _____ _____.

The Contentious Woman

An excellent wife is the crown of her husband,
But she who shames him is like rottenness in his bones.

Proverbs 12:4

A contentious woman is one who is looking for a fight, who is always right, who never speaks words of respect to her husband, and who is not filled with the Spirit of God. Look at these verses from Proverbs. Tell how these verses can be used in a practical way.

Proverbs 14:1: _____
_____

Proverbs 14:4: This one will take some thought. Think about how people are more important than things. _____
_____
_____

Proverbs 18:22: _____
_____

Proverbs 19:13: _____
_____

Proverbs 19:14: _____
_____

Proverbs 21:9: _____
_____

Proverbs 21:19: _____
_____

Proverbs 27:15-16: _____

_____

There is no excuse for contention. Your hormones may be flying all over the place, the toilet may have overflowed, the kids may be fighting, there may not be enough money to cover the bills, but your response will come from your heart.

Don't take your frustration out on others, rather pour it out in prayer to your Heavenly Father. To keep from being contentious, be in the Word constantly praying and praising God for His goodness, encouraging your husband, and bringing joy and unity to the home.

Romans 12:18 says, "If possible, so far as it depends on you, be at peace with all men." What can you do to bring peace to your home? _____

_____

Questions to think about:

1. Are you a contentious woman?

2. If your answer to #1 is yes, what are you going to do to change this?

3. Is it okay to be contentious during your period or menopause?

4. Work on your memory verse, Proverbs 3:13-26.

     How …
     For her …
     She is …
     Long life …
     Her ways …
     She is …
     The Lord …
     By His …
     My son …
     So they …
     Then you …
     And your …
     When you …
     When you …
     Do not …
     Nor of …
     For the…
     And will …

Week 7 Group Discussion

1. What does it mean to be prudent? (acting with or showing care and thought for the future. You might ask to give some examples of prudent behavior in a marriage.)

2. Why is it important to your marriage to keep growing closer to God?

3. Why does Christian marriage matter to our culture and its view of God?

4. Can someone work and make home a priority?

5. What might someone gain by being a worker at home?

6. Are you a godly woman according to the lists?

7. Do you know a godly man according to these lists?

8. If you are married, how can you better support and encourage your husband?

9. What are some words of respect and appreciation you can speak to your husband?

10. Is it wrong to be beautiful and to enhance your looks with make up or pretty clothes?

11. How can you initiate changes into your communication patterns?

12. What are the characteristics of a contentious woman?

13. Recite Proverbs 3:13-26 together.

Wise Woman of Proverbs 31

Charm is deceitful and beauty is vain,
But a woman who fears the Lord,
She shall be praised.

Proverbs 31:30

Dressed for success, professionally combed and curried, making homemade meals for her perfectly behaved children, running the women's ministry at the church between appointments for her career, and having time and energy for an incredible sex life with her husband may be your image of the perfect woman.

John McArthur describes the composite woman of our time in his commentary on the Proverbs 31 woman:

> What is it our society really views as the woman to be exalted? The woman
> to be honored? What is the excellent woman of the nineties [and the 21st century]
> really look like? What kind of woman is she? What is the modern superwoman?

> Well I suppose if we created a composite it might go a little like this. She works,
> builds her career, demands equal pay, refuses to submit to her husband, demanding
> equality with him in everything. Has an affair or two and a divorce or two. Exercises
> her independence. Relies on her own resources. Doesn't want her husband or her
> children to threaten her personal goals. Very often has her own bank account.
> She hires a maid or a cleaning service, eats out at least 50 percent of the time
> with her family or without. Makes cold cereal and coffee the standard
> breakfast for everybody. Quick frozen meals, the usual dinner fare if there
> is a dinner fare at home. Expects her husband to do at least an equal share
> of housework. She is tanned, coiffured, aerobicized, shopping to keep up
> the fashion trends, make sure she can compete in the attention-getting contest.
> She puts the kids in a day-care center. Makes sure each one has a TV in his
> room or a radio and a CD player so they are entertained all the time and

don't bother her … leaving them to the brainwashing of the immoral
materialistic society that pumps whatever it pumps through those media.
She is opinionated, usually, likes to be heard from and is eager to fulfill her
personal goals.

That's the kind of woman that the world applauds. She can't really stay married,
can't stay happy and her kids get into trouble and sometimes drugs and often
become criminals. And she is far from the woman that God has called the excellent woman to be.[44]

Who does God consider to be a woman of worth? Read Proverbs 31:10-31.

The Proverbs 31 woman seems perfect. The best commentary I ever heard on Proverbs 31 was that the writer was from the perspective of a woman who was older and looking back on her life. In the different seasons of life, she was able to accomplish all of the tasks–not all at once! Talk about one tired lady! She was only able to accomplish it all throughout her lifetime because of her relationship with God.

Let's look at these wonderful verses which are actually a poem written by King Lemuel. By the general consent of Jewish and Christian writers, this was probably another name for Solomon. *Lemuel* means "dedicated to or belonging to God."[45] If the writer was Solomon, he could be honoring Bathsheba, his mother, with his words.

Look at verse 10. What is an excellent wife compared to? _____

Notice she is not just as good as fine jewels, but her worth is far above jewels! What else in your study of Proverbs was compared to jewels? _____ (Prov. 3:13-15).

We can infer from this that an excellent wife has biblical wisdom. Jewels have a greater worth than just their beauty. They have the innate worth of a precious stone. They are sought after, bargained over, traded, and horded. So should a woman of worth be to her husband. She should bring a great wealth of knowledge, industry, and wisdom into the relationship.

Verse 11 talks about trust. It is so important in the marriage relationship for both parties to be able to trust the other. This means open and honest conversation. Honor your spouse in your words to others. Don't get into the trap of one upping your companions. Commit to keep secret and between the two of you your sex life and your emotional intimacy. Protect one another. Proverbs 31 says this will bring great gain. If you have not been a trustworthy spouse in the past, you can start now and show your husband he can trust you. In verse 12, the excellent wife has what kind of actions for her husband? _____

These actions are not reactionary, but take the initiative–the initiative to serve him with meals, a clean house, and clean clothes; the initiative to massage his tired muscles or to kidnap him from work for a picnic. (Marriage can be a lot of fun!) Having an attitude of service can help to keep respect and calm seas in a marriage. Seeking to serve your husband keeps your mind off of yourself and your needs. When you serve, he will likely respond with appreciation, service, and approval.

Men have the responsibility by God to provide for and protect his family and home. But don't shrug off the woman's ability to influence her husband. If you want a voice of influence in your home, be a servant, a partner, and a friend. The husband may be the head, but it can only move because the neck, the wife, allows it!

Verses 13 and 14 seem odd for our culture. Today it would read, "She shops for clothes that will enhance his looks, and delights in washing and ironing them with her hands. She gathers food from the market and feeds her family well." [My version].

The wise woman finds contentment in serving her husband. Is your life so fast paced, you get frustrated if your husband asks you to iron a shirt? Or do you expect him to do it himself or send it out to be done? There is a satisfaction in slowing down and doing little things for your husband with your own hands. It can be a time for reflection and prayer, a time for gratefulness and thanksgiving. God gave you this man for a lifetime companion. Take the time to appreciate him.

Feeding my family well has always been a challenge for me. I was not allowed to help in the kitchen as a child, except to occasionally make cookies. I came into marriage knowing how to make cookies and bread. That was it! I exploded hard boiled eggs and made clumpy oatmeal and soggy French toast. Instead of giving up and seeking prepared foods, I kept at it and became an adequate cook. Meal planning is still my bane. It takes real discipline for me to have a week's worth of meals planned, shopped for, and prepared. But my kids never went hungry.

What area of homemaking is challenging for you? _____ . What can you do to improve?

_____

Questions to think about:

1. What is your favorite jewel? Do you own one?

2. How can you garner trust from your husband? (Singles: do your friends consider you trust worthy? What can you do to show that trust?)

3. What chores of goodness can you begin to do for your husband? (Singles: for a friend?)

4. What attitude do you need to acquire to serve your husband better? (Singles: to serve others better?)

5. Use this week to solidify your memory verses. If you have come across another Proverb which really spoke to your heart, try memorizing it as well.

    How …
    She is …
    Her ways …
    The Lord …

My son …
Then you …
When you …
Do not …
Nor of …
For the…
And will …

Woman's Work and Wealth

She rises also while it is still night
And gives food to her household
And portions to her maidens.

Proverbs 31:15

Read Proverbs 31:15-19. Use this example of godly womanhood to encourage you to reach new heights. Don't let it frustrate and depress you.

Verse 15 tells of the godly woman's untiring love and the priority she places on her home. She is not lazy. Laziness will lead to ruin, disrespect, contentions, and slovenliness in dress and home. I don't think I hardly ever sit down during the day at home. There is so much to do. Keeping a house organized and cleaned, laundry caught up, shopping done, and necessary phone calls made takes up much of the day. When you add children or grandchildren to the mix as well as ministry and work, your head can spin. Keeping organized is the key to successfully running a household.

Organization comes easy to some, but to others it can be a real challenge. Just as cooking was my challenge, if organization is yours, there is no excuse for not learning and practicing it. Start by putting like things with like things, having a place for everything, and purging the items you no longer need. Develop systems such as laundry rules and schedules. Laundry should never be on the floor. It should go from drawer to body to clothes basket to washer to dryer to dresser. Regular weekly meal plans for breakfasts and lunches can be a help: Monday—pancakes, Tuesday—oatmeal, Wednesday—cereal, etc.

Once you get a plan in place, follow through and make it a habit. Even if you are just trying to put your purse in the same place every day instead of always scrambling around trying to find it, it will take close to a month of practice before it becomes habit.

Read verse 16. "She considers a field and _____ it; from her _____ she plants a vineyard."

The Proverbs 31 woman is a good business woman who is responsible with the family finances. Some have to work outside of the home, others are able to stay at home and through thrift and hard work make ends meet. Whether God has called you to a career or job or to stay at home, do it whole-heartedly as unto the Lord.

Again, have a plan and carry it out. Be careful of frivolously spending money. If you decide you need something not in your budget, wait a day or two. If you still really need it, then figure out what you can do without to purchase the necessity. Usually, after a couple of days, I realize it was a want and not a need.

Having a cottage industry is a great way to stay home and earn money. Sewing, baking, teaching a skill, cleaning other's homes, selling a product, working from a home office or computer, or watching someone else's child are all possible ways of earning money while staying home. Some who work outside of the home are still able to keep home a priority and provide a comfortable and restful place for their families.

What can you do to earn extra income while making your home your priority? _____
_____
_____

Verse 17 says, "She girds herself with _____ and makes her arms strong." I don't think this means she spends all of her time at the gym! Balance in all things. She does make sure she is getting enough exercise so her body is healthy and strong. She takes care of herself. She exercises regularly and stays fit. What do you do for exercise? _____
_____

Even walking a mile a day will increase your stamina and give you more energy for your daily tasks.

This verse also speaks of strength of character which comes from growing in her walk with Jesus. What spiritual exercise are you doing daily to strengthen your faith? _____

Verse 18 speaks of the contentment and self-fulfillment a woman gains by doing her job well. "She senses that her gain is _____; her lamp does not go out at night." This woman is able to burn the candle at both ends. Although needing eight hours of sleep at night is not sinful, being able to adjust your schedule to perform your tasks well is wise. Know how much sleep you need to function at full capacity and plan for that amount.

The fact that she sees results from her labor motivates her to work into the night at times. Last minute science projects or a husband who comes home late discouraged may require patience and selflessness. She offers this with a quiet and gentle spirit, ready to serve, and eager to help.

Verse 19 again tells of her prowess with household responsibilities. You no longer have to make your own thread to weave your own clothes (the distaff and the spindle were used for preparing the thread and weaving the cloth), but you should be learning and growing in areas of meal planning and preparation, laundry, even gardening and canning, knitting or sewing.

I shared before that when God handed out the computer chips, I was not in the line for the cooking chip. I have a magnet on my refrigerator which claims the only reason I have a kitchen is because it came with the house!

I would much rather be writing or teaching. But I have muddled through, read cookbooks, tried a few new things, and managed to feed a family of seven for years. Now, baking bread and brownies? I am your woman for that! Unfortunately, man cannot live on bread and brownies alone! Try something new, you might find you like it!

Questions to think about:

1. How much sleep do you need?

2. What needs to be organized at your house?

3. What homemaking skill can you learn and employ for the good of others?

4. Bone up on your memory verses, Proverbs 3:13-26.

> How …
> She is …
> Her ways …
> The Lord …
> My son …
> Then you …
> When you …
> Do not …
> Nor of …
> For the…
> And will …

A Wise Woman's Sphere of Influence

She extends her hand to the poor,
and she stretches out her hands to the needy.

Proverbs 31:20

They say that man is mighty,
 He governs land and sea,
 He wields a mighty sceptre,
 O'er lesser powers that be,
 But a mightier power and stronger,
 Man from his throne has hurled,
 For the hand that rocks the cradle,
 Is the hand that rules the world.[46]

What is your sphere of influence? Begin today's lesson by reading Proverbs 31:20-23, 28.

List the people the Proverbs 31 woman influences for good.
  1.
  2.
  3.
  4.

Verse 20 shows the generosity of an excellent wife. She is able from her abundance because of her careful management of the house, to share with those less fortunate. It's really fun to see someone in need of food and buy them groceries, leave them on their front porch, and run. They only know that God supplied (you were His servant). It is fun to make up Christmas baskets for a family who lost their job. Helping others is being a great example to your kids. They can get into the spirit of things by reading to an older adult or playing a board game with a neighbor who can't get out much. Use your imagination and pray for opportunities to help others.

We, as Christian women, have the awesome ability to influence many. What are your spheres of influence? Start

with the people in your home and work outwards._____
_____
_____
_____

Verses 21-24 speaks of her ability to not only clothe her family and any other members of her household, but to do it well. They are wearing garments of purple and scarlet which were only worn by royalty. Remember, you are a daughter of the King, your husband is a prince, and your children little princes and princesses! Even if you can't afford expensive clothing, they can be neat and well cared for. Teach your children to clothe themselves in honor and humility, contentment and joy—no matter what their outer garments may be!

What does Colossians 3:12-13 say you should put on?

     1.

     2.

     3.

     4.

     5.

     6.

     7.

Attire yourself with these and you will be wise. Add to them the garments of Proverbs 31:25.
"_____ and _____ are her clothing, and she smiles at the future."

Strength and dignity causes this godly woman to not be afraid of the future.

Where does the strength and dignity come from? Her relationship with God and her husband. Spiritual strength will gird you with dignity no matter in what circumstances you find yourself. A solid loving relationship with your husband will gird you with confidence and fearlessness.

In verse 26 what two things also come from this same source? _____
_____

You do not have to be a teacher to teach with wisdom and kindness. These attributes are caught as you teach them with your actions. A life lived well is the best teacher of all.

Questions to think about:

    1. What household chore seems hard for you to accomplish?

    2. What's your plan to get better at this task?

    3. What steps can you take to becoming a woman of positive influence?

4. Really think about the message behind Proverbs 3:13-26 as you recite them today.

How ...
She is ...
Her ways ...
The Lord ...
My son ...
Then you ...
Do not ...
Nor of ...
For the...
And will ...

The Fear of the Lord

She looks well to the ways of her household,
And does not eat the bread of idleness.

Proverbs 31:27

et's finish up this great passage on a woman's work and worth. Read verse 27-31. Underlying all of Proverbs 31 woman's activities is what motivation? _____
_____

This takes you in a full circle from the beginning of this Proverbs study. You learned in Proverbs 1:7, "The fear of the Lord is the beginning of _____." In Psalms 111:10, you find, "The fear of the Lord is the beginning of _____." What is this fear of the Lord?

The fear of the Lord comes when you acknowledge your sin and seek God. The more you know Him, the more you fear Him because He is just, holy, righteous, and perfect, and He holds your future in His hands. Now, if you are without unconfessed sin, then you do not need to fear God. He is a loving parent who will discipline you, but He wants to be reconciled with you so you can have an intimate relationship with Him. You should fear His wrath if you are disobeying Him, and you should reverence Him always.

Think of it this way. If you just robbed a bank and are running away from the crime scene and you see a policeman, you will be afraid of him because you know he could put you away in prison for a long time. You understand he is your judge and you fear his capturing you. But if you are out on a picnic with your family, and you have committed no crime, and you see a policeman you might walk right up to him and say "Hi." You respect and reverence the policeman, but you have no fear of reprisal.

The Bible talks about this in the book of Romans. Read Romans 13:3-4. Your righteousness came through the blood of Jesus Christ. You will have no fear of _____ from God (Romans 8:1). When you remember this and live accordingly, you, too, can walk with confidence and joy in the fear of the Lord.

Verse 28 tells you of the Proverbs 31 woman's reward. This verse always reminds of the time one of my children threw some words back into my face. When they would fuss over doing chores, I would tell them that someday they would bow down and call me blessed. One day, as I stepped out of the bathroom, my eight-year old ran through the hallway, threw himself down at my feet, clasped his hands in front of him and yelled "Blessed". He then jumped up and ran outside. I called him back in to find out what he was doing. He said, "You're always saying that one day I will bow down and call you blessed, well I thought I would do it now and get it over with." He is now 26 and has a much better understanding of what this phrase means. He often thanks me for the lessons he learned and the discipline which he received. He is a fine young man.

Have your children called you blessed? Maybe not in those words, but have they thanked you for all you do? Do they honor you with conversation and love?

Praise from the wise woman's husband is her other reward. What greater joy can a woman have than for her husband to brag about her to others? He holds her in high esteem. He recognizes her worth! She will walk on clouds for days after her beloved repeats such praises to his friends or family. She has earned it. It is not flattery, it is truth. She has spent time with her God, used her gifts wisely, loved her husband and children well, been kind to others, and she is at peace with herself, content and joyful.

Verse 31 says that the works of her hands speak for themselves of her greatness. When people say we have done a great job raising our five boys, my response is that the proof is in the pudding and the pudding is not done yet. Well, the pudding is almost finished, and I am proud of five young men who love God, desire to raise godly children, and are a joy and a blessing to their Mom and Dad.

What praises do you receive from the work of your hands? _____
_____

Questions to think about:

1. Have you called your mother blessed? Now would be a good time!

2. Have your children called you blessed?

3. Does your husband praise you? What does he praise you for?

4. Last time! Recite Proverbs 3:1-26 aloud.

Week 8 / Day 5

Your Story Through the Names of God

The Lord is my Shepherd.

Psalm 23:1

How would you fill out the rest of this statement?
God is… _____

_____

The God of the Bible is so many things to his children as revealed by His many names. As God revealed Himself and different aspects of His character to his children in the Old Testament, He revealed another one of His names. As they walked through their lives, God revealed more and more to them about His character.

Here are some of His names:

Adonai —   (Lord, plural) The One high and above all things; the Owner of all there is; Lord and Master

Elohim —   El-unlimited strength, energy, might, and power Alah-to swear, declare or make a covenant.

Therefore, Elohim —   to the covenanted ones, I AM a supply of strength, energy, might, and power. He is totally dependable.

El-Shaddai —   (God Almighty) Giver and Sustainer of life.

El-Elyon —   (Most High God) The Possessor of heaven and earth; Omnipotent; the Strongest Strong One.

El-Olam —   (The everlasting God) eternal duration, everlasting, evermore. God's timelessness, His vast knowledge and His constancy and stability.

El-Roi –	(The God Who Sees) One who watches over us, concerning Himself with our needs.
Jehovah –	(Lord God) "He who is truly present"; eternal; Self-existent.
Jehovah-Jireh –	(The Lord Will Provide) Ultimately through Jesus Christ.
Jehovah-Nissi –	(The Lord is My Banner) All power is with Him; all strength comes from Him; our victory.
Jehovah-Tsidkenu –	(The Lord Our Righteousness) The only truly righteous One; the absolute, impeccable standard.
Jehovah-Roah –	(The Lord is My Shepherd) One tending, pasturing, leading, feeding, and protecting very dependent creatures.[47]

You learn to relate to different aspects of God as you grow as a Christian. I first accepted God as God the Creator, then God of history and the Bible. Later I accepted Him as my Savior. Soon He began being my Lord in all areas of my life. It took a while, but eventually He became my shepherd as I trusted Him with my provision and protection. He became my King, and I would do anything for Him out of obedience. Soon after this, He became my Friend. I could walk with Him, talk with Him, and tell Him anything. I knew He was always there. Lastly, for me, He became my Heavenly Father. I could sit in His lap and fully trust Him. I am not to the point of understanding God fully as my Bridegroom, but as I fellowship with Him daily, I pray that time will come. It is a journey. It was painful at times as God revealed my pride, or sinfulness, or unbelief to me, but always He was there to heal the wounds and claim Himself Sufficient in all things!

How has God revealed Himself to you? Not in your intellect but experientially? Where has your journey taken you and where do you need to head? Take a few minutes and write out the names of God as He revealed Himself to you. Meditate on the names of God and rejoice over your victories!

Circle the names of God which are an experiential reality in your life and then move forward to claim others as well.

Faithful	Forgiving	Salvation	Master and Lord
Source of Strength	Shelter	Creator	Architect and Builder
Defender	King of Kings	Father	God Almighty
My Rock	God of Grace	God of Hope	God of Love
God of Peace	The Truth	The Life	Holy Father
The Great Physician	God Who is There	Provider	Protector

Comforter	Shepherd	Friend	All Sufficient One
The Potter	Alpha and Omega	Bridegroom	Refuge
Judge	Anchor		

Pray about the names you did not circle. Ask God to reveal Himself to you as each of these.

I hope you have enjoyed this journey through Proverbs. I will leave you with James 1:5.

> "But if any of you lacks wisdom, let him ask of God, who gives to all generously and without reproach, and it will be given to him."

Questions to think about:

1. Choose a couple of God's names and share how He has shown Himself faithful in these areas in your life.

2. Spend some time in prayer praising God for who He is, thanking Him for His good gifts, and laying any encumbrances at His feet. Pray that God will reveal Himself to you in new and exciting ways.

Week 8 Group Discussion

1. What is your favorite jewel? Do you own one? How is a good wife like a jewel?

2. How can you garner trust from your husband? (Singles: do your friends consider you trust worthy? What can you do to show that trust?)

3. What attitude do you need to acquire to serve your husband better? (Singles: to serve others better?)

4. What needs to be organized at your house?

5. What steps can you take to becoming a woman of positive influence?

6. Does your husband praise you? What does he praise you for?

7. Choose a couple of God's names and share how He has shown Himself faithful in these areas in your life.

8. Recite Proverbs 3:13-26 together.

Proverbs 3:13-26 (NASB)

13 How blessed is the man who finds wisdom
And the man who gains understanding.

14 For her profit is better than the profit of silver
And her gain better than fine gold.

15 She is more precious than jewels;
And nothing you desire compares with her.

16 Long life is in her right hand;
In her left hand are riches and honor.

17 Her ways are pleasant ways
And all her paths are peace.

18 She is a tree of life to those who take hold of her,
And happy are all who hold her fast.

19 The Lord by wisdom founded the earth,
By understanding He established the heavens.

20 By His knowledge the deeps were broken up
And the skies drip with dew.

21 My son, let them not vanish from your sight;
Keep sound wisdom and discretion,

22 So they will be life to your soul
And adornment to your neck.

23 Then you will walk in your way securely
And your foot will not stumble.

24 When you lie down, you will not be afraid;
When you lie down, your sleep will be sweet.

25 Do not be afraid of sudden fear
Nor of the onslaught of the wicked when it comes;

26 For the Lord will be your confidence
And will keep your foot from being caught.

Appendix B

Recommended Reading:

Carter, Les. *The Anger Workbook*. Nashville: Thomas Nelson, 1993.

Carter, Les. *The Choosing to Forgive Workbook*. Nashville: Thomas Nelson, 1997.

Carter, Les and Frank Minirth. *The Anger Trap*. Jossey-Bass, 2004.

Chapman, Gary. *The Five Love Languages*. Chicago: Northwood Publishing, 2015.

Chapman, Gary and Ross Campbell. *The Five Love Languages of Children*. 3 ed. Chicago: Northwood Publishing, 2012.

Cloud, Henry and John Townsend. *Boundaries: When to Say Yes, When to Say No —To Take Control of Your Life*. Grand Rapids: Zondervan, 1992.

Colson, Chuck. *How Now Shall We Live?* Wheaton, IL: Tyndale House Publishers, 2004.

Cooper, Darian B. *You Can Be the Wife of a Happy Husband: Discovering the Keys to Marital Success*. St. Louis: Destiny Image Publishing, 2011.

DeMoss, Nancy L. *Surrender: The Heart God Controls*. Chicago, IL.: Moody Publishing, 2003.

Dillow, Linda. *Creative Counterpart*. Nashville: Thomas Nelson, 1977.

Eggerichs, Dr. Emerson. *Cracking the Communication Code*. Nashville: Thomas Nelson, 2008.

Eggerichs, Dr. Emerson. *Love & Respect: The Love She Most Desires, The Respect He Desperately Needs*. Nashville: Thomas Nelson, 2004.

Elliott, Elizabeth. *Passion and Purity: Learning to Bring Your Love Life Under Christ's Control. Grand Rapids:* Fleming H. Revell, 2002.

Erickson-Tada, Joni and Steve Estes. *When God Weeps: Why Our Suffering Matters to the Almighty.* Grand Rapids: Zondervan, 1997.

Freed, Jeffrey and Laurie Parsons. *Right-Brained Kids in a Left-Brained World: Unlocking the Potential of your ADD Child.* New York: Simon & Schuster, 1988.

Gillham, Anabel. *The Confident Woman: Knowing Who You Are in Christ.* Eugene, Oregon: Harvest House, 1993.

Gresh, Dannah. *And the Bride Wore White.* Chicago: Moody Publishers, 2004.

Halydier, Dara. *As They Sit and Stand: A Resource and Guide for Teaching Your Children the Bible.* Brownwood, TX: TD Publishing, 2014.

Halydier, Dara. *Living Beautifully: Practical Proverbs for Women Book 1.* Brownwood, TX: TD Publishing, 2018.

Harley, William F. *His Needs, Her Needs.* Grand Rapids: Fleming H. Revell, 2001.

Katherine, Anne. *Boundaries: Where You End and I Begin.* Center City, MN: Hazelden, 1991.

Kilgo, Edith Flowers. *Handbook for Christian Homemakers.* Grand Rapids: Baker Book House, 1982.

Lewis, C.S. *Mere Christianity.* London: Macmillan Publishers, 1952.

Lord, Peter. *Hearing God.* Grand Rapids: Baker Book House, 1988.

Ludy, Eric. *When God Writes Your Love Story.* Colorado Springs: Multnomah, 2004.

Martin, Bekah Hamrick. *The Bare Naked Truth: Dating, Waiting, and God's Purity Plan.* Grand Rapids: Zondervan, 2013.

McGee, Robert. *The Search for Significance.* Nashville: W Publishing Group, 2003.

McGee, Robert, Jim Craddock, and Pat S. McGee. *The Parent Factor.* Nashville: Rapha Publishing, 1989.

Moore, Beth. *Believing God.* Nashville: B&H Publishing Group, 2004.

Ortlund, Anne. *Children are Wet Cement.* Grand Rapids: Fleming H. Revell, 1978.

Ortlund, Anne. *Disciplines of a Beautiful Woman.* Waco: Word Books, 1984.

Parrott, Les and Leslie Parrott. *Saving Your Marriage Before It Starts.* Grand Rapids: Zondervan, 2006.

Paulsen, Heather. *Emotional Purity.* Wheaton, IL: Crossway Books, 2007.

Scazzero, Peter. *Emotionally Healthy Spirituality.* Nashville: Zondervan, 2014.

Schaeffer, Francis. *The Mark of a Christian.* Westmont, IL: Intervarsity Press, 2006.

Silvious, Jan. *Foolproofing Your Life.* New York City: Doubleday Religious Publishing Group, 1998.

Sire, James W. *The Universe Next Door.* Intervarsity Press, 1994.

Thomas, Gary L. *Sacred Marriage: What if God Designed Marriage to Make Us Holy More Than to Make Us Happy.* Nashville: Zondervan, 2002.

Thurman, Dr. Chris. *The Lies We Believe.* Nashville: Thomas Nelson Publishers, 1989.

Leader's Guide

Week 1

Week 1 / Day 1: History of Pride

Look up Mark 7:21-23. Listed among this infamous group of sins is pride.
Where do these verses say pride comes from? __**from within, out of the heart of men**__

According to Isaiah 14:11 what led to Satan's downfall? __**his pomp**__

In verse 13 you can see the intent of his heart. "But you said in __**your**__ __**heart**__, 'I will ascend to heaven; I will raise my throne above the stars of God, and I will sit on the mount of assembly in the recesses of the north. I will ascend above the heights of the clouds; I will make myself like the Most High.'"

What has your pride cost you? __**Answers will vary**__
Has your pride kept you from making a commitment to Jesus Christ? __**Answers will vary**__
Has your pride brought heartache to others and severed their trust? __**Answers will vary**__
Has your pride destroyed opportunities to serve God? __**Answers will vary**__

Questions to think about:

1. How can you overcome this pride? **Answers will vary**

2. Are you willing to give it a try? **Answers will vary**

Week 1 / Day 2: God's Thoughts About Pride

According to Proverbs 8:13, what are God's thoughts about pride? __**He hates it**__

Look at what God says about pride, arrogance, boasting, haughtiness, and trusting in yourself. James 4:16 says, "But as it is, you boast in your arrogance; all such boasting is __**evil**__."

Look up Proverbs 6:16-19. God hates six things and seven things are an abomination to Him. What is the first on the list? __**haughty eyes**____. That's pride!

Proverbs 21:4 says: "Haughty eyes and a proud heart, the lamp of the wicked, is __**sin**____."

Does God take pride seriously? The Scriptures say He hates pride. Why do you think this is? __**Answers will vary. Pride keeps us from seeing our need of relationship with God. It elevates our view of ourselves, thus lowering our view of God**_____

2 Corinthians 3:5 reminds you, "Not that we are adequate in __**ourselves**____ to consider anything as coming from ourselves, but our adequacy is from __**God**_____."

He is your breath, your life, your very being. You are to work with Him, but never forget that without Him you can do nothing (John 15:5). This applies to all men. Look at John 1:3. "All things came into being through Him (Jesus), and apart from Him __**nothing**_____ came into being that has come into being. In Him was life."

1 Corinthians 8:6: "For us there is but one God, the Father from whom are ____**all**____ things and we exist __**for**____ Him; and one Lord Jesus Christ, by whom are ___**all**___ things, and we exist __**through**__ Him."

Colossians 1:16 -17: "For by Him __**all**__ things were created, both in the heavens and on earth, visible and invisible, whether thrones or dominions or rulers or authorities – __**all**____ things have been __**created**_____ __**through**_____ Him and __**for**____ Him. He is before all things, and in Him __**all**_____ things hold together."

To finish up today's lesson, look at Proverbs 25:27. What are God's thoughts about pride? "It is not good to eat much honey, nor is it glory to search out one's own __**glory**_____."

Proverbs 27:2 says, "Let another praise you, and __**not**____ your own mouth; A stranger, and __**not**___ your own lips."

Because God hates pride, He has placed a judgment on it. Read Proverbs 16:5. "Everyone who is proud in heart is an abomination to the Lord; assuredly, he will not be __**unpunished**_____."

God further declares in Isaiah 13:11, "I will also put an end to the __**arrogance**_____ of the proud and abase the __**haughtiness**_____ of the ruthless."

Questions to think about:

1. What is your self-esteem based upon (looks, performance, or others opinions)? **Answers will vary**

2. What should your self-esteem be based upon? **You are a daughter of the King of Kings and He loves you unconditionally.**

3. How does this help you to avoid pride? **My value is not based on what I do, how I look, or what others think about me. All that I have is from God.**

4. Start memorizing Proverbs 3:13-14.

How blessed is the man who finds __**wisdom**__
And the man who gains __**understanding**__.
For her profit is better than the profit of __**silver**__,
And her gain is better than fine __**gold**__.

Week 1 / Day 3: Being Humble

Read Romans 12:16. "Be of the __**same**__ mind toward one another; do not be __**haughty**__ in mind, but associate with the __**lowly**__. Do not be __**wise**__ in your own estimation."

Do you tend to be judgmental of someone who does things differently from you? _____

When was the last time you were squeezed by life's circumstances? __**Answers will vary**__
What was your response?
  a.) hurt and anger
  b.) self-pity
  c.) arrogance
  d.) humility and concern for others

Proverbs 22:4 __**riches, honor, and life**__

Proverbs 21:29 __**a sure way**__

Proverbs 18:12 and Proverbs 15:33 __**honor**__

How do you compare with the six characteristics of a humble person? __**Answers will vary**__

Questions to think about:

1. How do you compare to each of the definitions of humility? **Answers will vary**

2. Overall, would you say you have an attitude of pride or humility? In what areas do you need to work on becoming more humble? **Possible answers: relationships, work, sports, choir, etc...**

3. Practice memorizing Proverbs 3:13-14.

    How __**blessed**__ is the man who finds __**wisdom**__
    And the man who gains __**understanding**__.
    For her __**profit**__ is better than the profit of __**silver**__,
    And her __**gain**__ is better than fine __**gold**__.

Week 1 / Day 4: Pride vs. Humility

But first, let's review. What is the opposite of pride? __**humility**__

List 6 characteristics of a humble man from the last lesson.

1. **Has a good understanding of his relationship with God**
2. **Is grateful**
3. **Blesses his mother and father in word and action**
4. **Acknowledges when he sins and is quick to repent**
5. **Is content and satisfied with his lot in life**
6. **Is giving and compassionate towards others**

Here are some verses to look up:

Proverbs 11:2 "When pride comes, then comes __**dishonor**__, but with the humble is wisdom."

Proverbs 14:16 "A wise man is cautious and turns away from evil, but a fool is __**arrogant**__ and __**careless**__."

Proverbs 21: 24 "'Proud,' 'haughty,' 'scoffer,' are his names, who acts with __**insolent**__ pride."

List some of the characteristics of a prideful man according to these verses.

1. **dishonored**
2. **arrogant**
3. **careless**
4. **insolent**
5. **hopeless**
6. **wise in own eyes**
7. **scoffer or haughty**

Are you a grace giver? _____

Proverbs 27:2 "Let another __**praise**__ you and not your own mouth, a stranger and not your own lips."

Proverbs 25:6-7 "Do not claim honor in the presence of the king, and do not stand in the place of great men; For it is better that it be said to you, '__**Come**__ __**up**__ __**here**__,'than for you to be placed lower in the presence of the prince whom your eyes have seen. "'

Questions to think about:

1. If you boast, what should you boast in? (Jeremiah 9:23-24) **You should boast that you understand and know God, that He is the Lord who exercises lovingkindness, justice and righteousness on earth**

2. In what areas of life are you tempted to boast about yourself? **Answers will vary**

3. Practice memorizing Proverbs 3:13-14.

How __**Blessed**__ is the __**man**__ who finds __**wisdom**__,
And the man who __**gains**__ __**understanding**__.
For her __**profit**__ is __**better**__ than the __**profit**__ of __**silver**__,
And her __**gain**__ is better than fine __**gold**__.

Week 1 / Day 5: Humility Through Obedience

Is your self-esteem reliant upon performance, other's opinions, or the way you look? _____
_____

What should your self-esteem be based upon? __**The fact that you are a daughter of the King of Kings**__

And now that you know your position, you can bend your knees to the Lord and understand what Isaiah 55:8-9 means.

"For My __**thoughts**__ are not your __**thoughts**__,
Nor are your __**ways**__ My __**ways**__," declares the Lord.
"For as the heavens are higher than the earth,
So are My ways __**higher**__ than your ways
And My thoughts than your thoughts."

Write John 10:27. __**My sheep hear My voice, and I know them, and they follow Me**__

How vital is hearing God to you? __**Answers will vary**__

Can you recall a time in your life you heard God and didn't listen to Him? __**Answers will vary**__

What about a time you heard God call and you did listen? __**Answers will vary**__

In John 15:11 Jesus says, "These things [His commandments] I have spoken to you so that My joy may be in you, and that __**your**__ joy may be made full." As you listen and obey God's voice, you will find joy!

Objective	Whose assignment	Yolk broke	Yolk is whole
Don't break yolk	mine	**failure**	**success**
Don't break yolk	God's	**success**	**success**

Questions to think about:

1. What are some ways you hear God's voice? **Through the Bible, through a sermon, through song, quiet whisper, audible voice, desire within your heart, dream, vision, circumstances.**

2. Do you spend time during prayer to listen? **Answers will vary**

3. Are you quick to obey? **Answers will vary**

Week 1 Group Discussion

The following questions were posed after the lessons this past week. Take time to discuss the answers and ask for responses. Additional verses are listed which will give you, the teacher, more insight. These lists are not exhaustive. Feel free to pray and ask God for other verses which answer these questions for you. You can study these ahead of time and then either ask the students look them up during class or just refer to them as you speak. Some of the questions might be personal. Don't push for answers. Either give an answer from your experience or move on.

1. In what areas or relationships do you battle pride? (Mark 7:20-23, 1 John 2:16) **Answers will vary**

2. How can you overcome this pride? (Matthew 23:12, Matthew 18:23-35) **When you realize the depth of your transgressions and the extent of God's forgiveness and grace, who are you, then, to hold anything against another or raise yourself up above another. Pray that God will show you the depth of your own sin.**

3. What should your self-esteem be based upon? (Eph. 2:4-10, col. 1:13-23, 2:10, John 1:12) **I am a sinner, unworthy, but by the grace of God I have been saved and am now a child of God.**

4. What is your self-esteem based upon? (**answers may include: how I look, how others see me, how I perform, how I am accepted**)

5. How does a proper understanding of who God is and who you are in Christ help you avoid pride? **Knowing that a holy, perfect God has chosen to forgive you and love you and even to delight in you is humbling because you are a sinner, unworthy. It is Jesus' righteousness which covers you, not your own.**

6. In what areas of life are you tempted to boast about yourself? (Psalm 34:2, Proverbs 27:1-2, Proverbs 25:14, Jeremiah 9:23-24, 2 Corinthians 12:9, Hebrews 3:6, James 3:5) **Answers will vary**

7. What are some ways you hear God's voice? **Bible, preaching, music, His voice, gentle urgings, conscience, dreams, etc.**

8. Do you spend time during prayer to listen? **Answers will vary**

9. Are you quick to obey? (John 15:10, Acts 5:29, 5:32, Romans 6:16, 2 Corinthians 10:5, Hebrews 5:9, 1 Peter 1:22–ordering your thought life to be obedient to Christ Jesus). **Answers will vary**

Week 2

Week 2 / Day 1: Trusting in Riches

Several verses in Proverbs give you some clues about how you should look at money.
Look at Proverbs 30:7-10 above. What two things did the writer of Proverbs ask God for?
1. **Keep deception and lies from me.**
2. **Give me neither poverty or riches.**

In the above verses, what was the temptation of the rich? __**To deny God**__
What was the temptation of the poor? ____**to steal and profane God's name**____

Matthew 6:33 gives you Jesus' perspective on what you should consider. According to this verse what should
you seek? ___**His kingdom and His righteousness**___
What is the word *all* referring to in this verse? __**food, clothes**___

	Those Who Trust in Riches	The Righteous
Prov. 11:28	will fall	will flourish
Prov. 15:16	**treasure and turmoil**	fear of the Lord
Prov. 28:6	crooked	**integrity**
Prov. 16:8	**injustice**	righteousness
Prov. 11:4	no profit	**delivered from death**
Prov. 10:16	**punishment**	**life**
Prov. 28:20	punishment	**blessings**

You might have memorized Proverbs 3:1-12 in the first part of this study. Verses 5-6 says to "Trust in the
__**Lord**__ with all your heart and lean not unto your own understanding, in all your ways acknowledge
__**Him**__ and He will make your paths straight."

Questions to think about:

1. How important is money to you? **Answers will vary**

2. Do you put your trust in riches or God? **Answers will vary**

3. Have you ever had an experience of needing something you just couldn't afford, and God provided for you? **Answers will vary**

4. Are you rich and don't need God or poor and always worrying about where your next dollar will come from? **Answers will vary**

5. How can you begin to have a proper attitude about money? **By having a grateful heart through praise and prayer. By giving instead of receiving. By having a reasonable budget.**

Week 2 / Day 2: How Much Is Enough?

Paul says in Philippians 4:11-12 that he has learned to be content in what circumstances? __**In whatever circumstances he was in, with humble means and prosperity**_____

> Be anxious for nothing, but in _____**everything**_____ by prayer and
> supplication with __**thanksgiving**_ let your requests be made known to God.
> And the peace of God, which surpasses all comprehension, will guard
> your hearts and your minds in Christ Jesus.

You learned yesterday that you should first seek God's __**kingdom and righteousness**_____.

In Philippians 4:19 you read, "And my God will supply all your ____**needs**_____ according to His riches in glory in Christ Jesus."

Fear is the opposite of trust. If you have fear of the future, of how God is going to meet your needs, of not having enough, etc., then you are not trusting God. What do you fear? _____

He also told them in verse 14 to, "be __**content**_____ with your wages."

Hebrews 13:5 says, "Make sure that your character is free from the love of money, being __**content**_____ with what you have; for He Himself has said, 'I will never leave you, nor will I ever forsake you.'"

How does this perspective differ from the traditional Christian perspective? **This view realizes the earth is Satan's dominion and as Christians we still live here and suffer from all earthly troubles. Traditionally, Christians think God will protect them from all trouble. Many Christians believe God should not allow them to get sick or to have hardships, that if they have enough faith, then life will only yield blessings.**

Questions to think about:

1. What heart condition should you learn in regards to money? **Contentment**

2. Do you expect things to go well and blame God when they go wrong or do you expect things to go

wrong and praise God when they go right? **Answers will vary**

3. Who is the god of this world? Who wins in the end? **Satan is the god of this world. God wins in the end.**

4. Are you content in whatever circumstance life finds you in? **Answers will vary**

5. Work on memorizing Proverbs 3:12-15.

> She is more precious than ___**jewels**___; and ___**nothing**___ you desire compares with her.
> Long life is in her ___**right**___ hand;
> In her ___**left**___ hand are riches and honor.

Week 2 / Day 3: Greed

When you think of majestic, proud animals does the ant, the shephanim (a small rodent like a chipmunk), the locust, or the lizard come to mind? No. When you think of majesty and power, what animal do you think of? _**Answers will vary: Lion, elephant, bear**___ .

When you think about powerful people, who comes to mind? _**Answers will vary: Clinton, Obama, Trump, etc…**___

You may have written Donald Trump, Barak Obama, Oprah, Bill Gates. These are people who have riches and power on the national scene. But are these godly, wise people you should emulate? ___**No**___

28:11 "The rich man is wise in his ___**own**___ ___**eyes**___, But the poor who has ___**understanding**___ sees through him."

18:11 "A rich man's wealth is his strong city, and like a high wall in his own ___**imagination**___."

10:15 "The rich man's wealth is his ___**fortress**___, The ruin of the poor is their poverty."

Take a minute and list the things you are grateful for.

1. **Answers will vary**	6.	11.
2.	7.	12.
3.	8.	13.
4.	9.	14.
5.	10.	15.

Read what Proverbs 13:25 has to add; "The righteous has enough to satisfy his ___**appetite**___, but the stomach of the wicked is in need."

Proverbs 10:30 says, "The righteous will __**not**__ be shaken, but the wicked will not dwell in the land."

Proverbs 14:11 gives us confidence that: "The house of the wicked will be destroyed, but the tent of the upright will __**flourish**__."

Questions to think about:

1. What are your basic needs? **Food, water, shelter**

2. Has God provided for your needs? **Yes**

3. Tell of a time when God unexpectedly provided more than your needs financially or emotionally. **Answers will vary**

4. She is more ____**precious**____ than ____**jewels**____;
    And __**nothing**__ you __**desire**__ compares with her.
    Long __**life**__ is in her __**right**__ hand;
    In her __**left**__ hand are __**riches**__ and honor.

Week 2 / Day 4: Giving

	The World's Way	God's Way
Life:	Cling to it	Matthew 16:24-25
		deny self
		lose life
Material needs:	Get all you can	Matthew 6:33
		seek God's Kingdom first
Enemies:	Get revenge	Matthew 5:44
		love your enemies and pray for them
Money :	Get it, horde it	Matthew 6:19
		Luke 6:38
		don't store up money
		give it away
Relationships:	Independence	Matthew 18:3
		become like children

What might be something one must let go of in order to gain a right relationship with God?
Here are a few examples to get you started: sins, dreams, time.

Now you add a few more. __**Answers will vary: singleness, job aspirations, desire for family, health, addictions, self-image, husband, children, control, anxiety, right for vindication, right for____ justice, anger, time, career, hobby, money, need for security, house, etc...**__

Proverbs 29:7: "The righteous is concerned for the rights of the poor, the wicked does not __**understand**__ such concern."

Proverbs 22:9: "He who is generous will be blessed, for he gives some of his __**food**__ to the poor."

Proverbs 21:13: "He who shuts his ear to the cry of the poor, will also cry himself and not be __**answered**__."

Proverbs 19:17: "One who is gracious to a poor man lends to the __**Lord**__, And He will repay him for his good deed."

Proverbs 18:23: "The poor man utters supplications, but the rich man answers __**roughly**__."

Proverbs 17:5: "He who mocks the poor taunts his __**Maker**__; He who rejoices at calamity will not go unpunished."

Proverbs 14:31: "He who oppresses the poor taunts his Maker, but he who is __**gracious**__ to the needy honors Him."

Proverbs 11:25: "The generous man will be prosperous, and he who waters will himself be __**watered**__."

Questions to think about:

1. What are you holding onto that God is asking you to release to Him? **Answers will vary**

2. Can you trust God enough to let go, and trust Him to meet all your needs in His way?
   Answers will vary

3. How might you give to the poor? **Through ministries set up to help the poor, paying a doctor's bill, food pantry, helping out a shelter, giving material possessions, etc...**

4. Are you responsible for what someone does with that which you give them? **No. But we should give responsibly.**

5. Are you tithing? **Yes or No**

6. If your response is "No," which church or ministry will you begin to send your tithe?
   Answers will vary

7. She is more __**precious**__ than ___**silver**___;
   And __**nothing**__ you __**desire**__ __**compares**__ with her.
   Long __**life**__ is in her __**right**__ __**hand**__;
   In her __**left**__ hand are __**riches**__ and __**honor**__.

Week 2 / Day 5: False Balances, Surety, and Borrowing

Read Proverbs 16:11. Why are scales and balances of concern to God? __**Answers will vary: God is concerned about every area of our life; He wants to be Lord over all, and He is truthful. If we are honest with the little issues of life, we will tend to be honest with the larger issues..**__

> If there is a poor man with you, one of your brothers, in any of the
> towns in the land which the Lord your God is giving you, you shall
> not __**harden**__ your heart from your poor brother; but
> you shall __**freely**__ open your hand to him and shall __**generously**__
> lend him sufficient for his need in whatever he lacks …

Proverbs 22:26-27 warns, "Do not be among those who give pledges, among those who become guarantors for debts. If you have nothing with which to pay, why should he take your __**bed**__ from under you?"

Questions to think about:

1. What is the heart issue behind false balances? **Dishonesty, selfish ambition, greed**

2. Give an example you have come across about false measurements. **Answers will vary**

3. What is the heart issue in usury? **Greed, selfish ambition**

4. What is the heart issue in borrowing? **Fear, not trusting God for your needs, greed**

5. Give an example of how borrowing turned out to be a bad idea in your life. **Answers will vary**

Extra: How to Set Up a Budget

Proverbs 14:15 puts it this way: "The naïve believes everything, but a sensible man __**considers**__ his steps."

Luke 16:11 is a good reminder for you about how you should use your money. "Therefore if you have __**not**__ __**been**__ __**faithful**__ in the use of wealth, who will entrust the true riches to you?"

Week 2 Group Discussion

The following questions were posed after the lessons this past week. Take time to discuss the answers and ask for responses. Additional verses are listed which will give you, the teacher, more insight. These lists are not exhaustive. Feel free to pray and ask God for other verses which answer these questions for you. You can study these ahead of time and then either ask the students look them up during class or just refer to them as you speak. Some of the questions might be personal. Don't push for answers. Either give an answer from your experience or move on.

1. How important is money to you? Do you put your trust in riches or God? (1 Tim.6:10, Matt. 6:24) **Answers will vary**

2. How can you begin to have a proper attitude about money? (Eccl. 5:10, 1 Tim. 6:10, Phil. 4:11) **Recognize that it is God who provides for you through your ability to do a job, by opening the doors for your position at work, etc. Recognize that every penny is a gift from God. Recognize that we are stewards of God's finances. Practice being thankful for every earthly possession. Practice contentment and praise.**

3. What heart conditions should you learn in regards to money? (Phil. 4:11, 1 Thess. 5:18) **Contentment, Gratefulness**

4. Do you expect things to go well and blame God when they go wrong, or do you expect things to go wrong and praise God when they go right? (Romans 8:28) **Answers will vary**

5. Who is the god of this world? Who wins in the end? (Eph. 2:2, 2 Cor. 4:4, John 12:31, Romans 16:20, Rev. 20:1-3, 10) **Satan is the god of this world, but God wins in the end!**

6. Tell of a time when God unexpectedly provided more than your needs financially or emotionally. **Answers will vary**

7. What are you holding onto that God is asking you to release to Him? (Mark 12:14, Romans 6:13, 1 Cor. 6:12) **Answers will vary**

8. Are you responsible for what someone does with what you gave them? **No. We are to give responsibly, but what the receiver does with our gift is up to them. Always give with no strings attached.**

9. What is the heart issue behind false balances? **Greed, deceit, pride**

10. What is the heart issue in usury? **Greed, selfishness, pride**

11. What is the heart issue in borrowing? **Fear (the opposite of trusting God), greed, pride, unbelief**

Week 3

Week 3 / Day 1: History of Work

Genesis 2:15 says God put the man into the garden to "cultivate it and __**keep**__ it."

God does not put a priority on kinds of work, but He does tell you in 2 Thessalonians 3:10-11 "If anyone is not willing to work, then he is not to __**eat**__ either…"

(Deuteronomy 5:12-13). "Observe the Sabbath day to __**keep**__ __**it**__ __**holy**__ as the Lord your God commanded you. Six days you shall labor and do all your work, but the __**seventh**__ day is a Sabbath of the Lord your God; in it you shall not do any work."

Proverbs 21:17 reminds you, "He who __**loves**__ __**pleasure**__ will become a poor man; He who loves wine and oil will not become rich."

What type of work do you like to do best? Physical, social, or mental? _____

What type of physical work do you do?_____

What type of social work do you do? _____

What type of mental work do you do? _____

What do you do for recreation? _____

What would you say your work to play ratio is? _____

Questions to think about:

1. Do you tend to be a workaholic or do you tend to avoid work as much as possible? **Answers will vary**

2. What motivates you to work hard? **Answers will vary**

3. Are you more valuable in God's estimation if you work hard or not? **No, but there is great reward in obedience and we should be motivated to do good works not for salvation, but in gratitude for our salvation.**

Week 3 / Day 2: Planning Ahead

Who are these two people?
1. **builder**
2. **king**

1 Timothy 2:2 says, "To pray for those in authority so that we may lead a __**quiet**__ and __**peaceful**__ life in all godliness and dignity."

Psalm 138:8 says, "The Lord __**will**__ __**accomplish**__ what concerns me; Your lovingkindness, O Lord, is everlasting; Do not forsake the works of Your hands."

What does Philippians 4:6 tell you not to do? __**worry or be anxious**__
What does this verse tell you to do? __**give thanks, making your requests known to God**__
What is the result from this obedience? __**peace that passes understanding**__

Questions to think about:

1. Are you successful at making a short term work plan and accomplishing it? **Answers will vary**

2. What is your long term work plan? Does it include college, a new job, marriage, children, retirement, ministry? **Answers will vary**

3. Are you making a plan through prayer and trusting God to lead, guide, and direct? **Answers will vary**

4. Her ways are __**pleasant**__ ways
   And all her paths are __**peace**__.
   She is a tree of __**life**__ to those who take hold of her,
   And happy are all who hold her __**fast**__.

Week 3 / Day 3: Diligence

Proverbs 10:4: "The hand of the diligent makes __**rich**__."

Proverbs 12:11: "He who tills his land will have plenty of __**bread**__."

Proverbs 12:14: "The __**deeds**__ of a man's hands will return to him."

Proverbs 12:27: This verse implies that a diligent man will roast his __**prey**__. "The precious possession of a man is his __**diligence**__."

Proverbs 13:4: "The __**soul**__ of the diligent is made fat."

Proverbs 14:23: "In all __**labor**__ there is profit."

Proverbs 27:18: "He who tends the fig tree will __**eat**__ its fruit, and he who cares for his master will be __**honored**__."

Proverbs 28:19: "He who tills his land will have plenty of __**food**__, but he who follows empty pursuits will have poverty in plenty."

From these verses what would you say is the opposite of diligence? **laziness, foolishness**

Proverbs 27:23-27 is a warning. What is not forever? **riches**

Proverbs 12:11: Someone who pursues worthless things lacks what? **sense**

Proverbs 10:5: How will the son who sleeps in harvest act? **shamefully**

Proverbs 24:10: "If you are slack in the day of distress, your strength is **limited**."

Proverbs 18:9: A slack person is considered a brother or kin to one whom **destroys**.

Proverbs 20:13: What does a lazy person love? **sleep** What will this gain him? **poverty**

Proverbs 21:25-26: The result of a sluggard refusing to work is **death**.

Proverbs 20:4: Again, the sluggard does without because he will not **work**.

Proverbs 19:15: What will an idle man suffer? **hunger**

How does vinegar taste? **bitter, acidic**.

Is your home clean? **Answers will vary** Proverbs 26:13-16.

What is the sluggard compared to as he turns upon his bed? **a hinge**

Questions to think about:

1. Are you an excuse maker? **Answers will vary**

2. What's the most creative excuse you ever made up or heard? **Answers will vary**

3. What areas do you need to become more diligent in? **Answers will vary**

4. Are you diligent in your relationships? **Answers will vary**

5. What might you commit to doing to become more diligent in these areas? **Answers will vary**

6. Her **ways** are **pleasant** ways
   And all her **paths** are **peace**.
   She is a **tree** of **life** to those who take hold of her,
   And **happy** are all who hold her **fast**.

Week 3 / Day 4: God Promises the Holy Spirit

"If you then, being evil, know how to give good gifts to your children, how much more will your heavenly Father give __**the**__ __**Holy**__ __**Spirit**__ to those who ask?"

Proverbs 15:6: "Great wealth is in the house of the __**righteous**__, but trouble is in the income of the wicked."

Psalm 19:7-10: "The law of the Lord … the testimony of the Lord … The precepts of the Lord … the commandment of the Lord … the fear of the Lord … the judgments of the Lord … are more desirable than __**gold**__, yes, than much fine gold, Sweeter also than honey and the drippings of the honeycomb."

Let's review Proverbs 3:13-15: "How blessed is the man who finds __**wisdom**__ and the man who gains __**understanding**__. For her profit is better than the profit of __**silver**__ and her gain better than fine __**gold**__. She is more precious than __**jewels**__; and nothing you desire compares with her."

Questions to think about:

1. Have you ever felt you did not have enough faith because God did not seem to answer your prayer? **Answers will vary**

2. What three answers might a parent or God give if you ask for something? **Yes, No, Not now**

3. Describe a time when God told you no or to wait.

4. Her __**ways**__ are __**pleasant**__ __**ways**__
   And __**all**__ her __**paths**__ are __**peace**__.
   She is a __**tree**__ of __**life**__ to those who take __**hold**__ of her,
   And __**happy**__ are all who __**hold**__ her __**fast**__.

Week 3 / Day 5: Wealth and Welfare

1 Samuel 2:7 is a good reminder. "The Lord makes __**poor**__ and __**rich**__; He brings low, He also exalts."

Psalm 82:3-4 tells you to "Vindicate the __**weak**__ and fatherless; do justice to the __**afflicted**__ and __**destitute**__. Rescue the __**weak**__ and __**needy**__; Deliver them out of the hand of the wicked."

Who do you know who is truly in need? __**Answers will vary**__ What might you do to help them out? __**Just giving money is rarely the answer. Perhaps teaching a skill, or providing a meal, or discipling them.**__

Proverbs 22:22-23 says "Do not ___**rob**___ the poor because he is poor, or ___**crush**___ the afflicted at the gate; For the Lord will plead their case and take the life of those who rob them."

Proverbs 19:7 "All the ___**brothers**___ of a poor man hate him, how much more do his ___**friends**___ abandon him!"

Proverbs 11:24 says, "There is one who ___**scatters**___, and yet increases all the more, and there is one who ___**withholds**___ what is justly due, and yet it results only in want."

Proverbs 13:11: "Wealth obtained by fraud ___**dwindles**___, But the one who gathers by labor ___**increases**___ it."

Proverbs 15:27: "He who profits ___**illicitly**___ troubles his own house, but he who hates bribes will live."

Proverbs 11:18: "The wicked earns ___**deceptive**___ wages, but he who sows righteousness gets a ___**true**___ reward."

Proverbs 10:2: "Ill-gotten gains do not profit, but righteousness delivers from ___**death**___."

Proverbs 28:22: "A man with an evil eye hastens after wealth, and does not know that ___**want**___ will come upon him."

Proverbs 22:16: "He who oppresses the poor to make more for himself, or who gives to the ___**rich**___ will only come to poverty."

Questions to think about:

1. Are you tithing faithfully? ___**Answers will vary**___ If not, will you trust God and begin today?

2. How might you give above your tithe? **Answers will vary**

3. Should you discern and treat differently the poor and the lazy poor? How might you treat each group to give the best help? **We can help those who are working hard but can't get ahead by helping with repairs to house or car, paying a medical bill, bringing them a meal, providing for a particular need, etc. The lazy poor should be encouraged to work for their wages.**

Week 3 Group Discussion

The following questions were posed after the lessons this past week. Take time to discuss the answers and ask for responses. Additional verses are listed which will give you, the teacher, more insight. These lists are not exhaustive. Feel free to pray and ask God for other verses which answer these questions for you. You can study these ahead of time and then either ask the students look them up during class or just refer to them as you speak. Some of the questions might be personal. Don't push for answers. Either give an answer from your experience or move on.

1. Do you tend to be a workaholic or do you tend to avoid work as much as possible? (Matt. 21:28, Luke 5:5, John 5:17, Romans 16:6) **Answers will vary**

2. What motivates you to work hard? **Answers will vary, but possible answers are: compliments, words of affirmation, money, others opinions, self-esteem is wrapped up with my performance, obedience, God's commands and warnings about work.**

3. Are you more valuable in God's estimation if you work hard or not? (Eph. 1:3-13, 2:4-10) **No. Our value is not set by how hard we work, but rather that we are God's child. He does reward those who obey and are diligent though.**

4. What are your long range plans? Does it include college, a new job, marriage, children, retirement, ministry? **Answers will vary**

5. What's the most creative excuse you ever made up or heard? **Answers will vary**

6. What areas do you need to become more diligent in? (Romans 12:8, 11, Heb. 6:11, Peter 1:5) **Answers will vary**

7. What might you commit to doing to become more diligent in these areas? **Answers will vary, but may include: getting up earlier, setting goals and rewards, have an accountability partner, etc.**

8. Have you ever felt you did not have enough faith because God did not seem to answer your prayers? (Ps. 3:4, 20:6, 34:4, 65:5) **Answers will vary, but God says when we call out to Him, He hears us. He may be saying to wait or no or not that way. He knows what is best for you.**

9. Describe a time when God told you no or to wait. **Answers will vary**

10. Should you discern and treat differently the poor and the lazy poor? How might you treat each group to give the best help? **Yes. Those who are working or unable to work, we need to come alongside and either help them out financially or teach them skills to help them get a better job. Those who choose not to work because of laziness and easy government help, we should train and teach in the word and help them realize the need to work hard, or if they don't want to change, we should leave them to their own fate.**

Week 4

Week 4 / Day 1: Wise Words I

Matthew 12:34: "For the mouth speaks out of that which fills the __**heart**__."

"But I tell you that every careless __**word**__ that people speak, they shall give an accounting for it in the Day of Judgment. For by your __**words**__ you will be justified, and by your __**words**__ you will be condemned."

Circle the following statements which mirror a heart seeking to please God.

Well done!   **You are so special to me**   **I love you**

Way to go!   Can't you do anything right?   **I am God's precious child**

I can't believe you did that, you moron!   I am no good.   You idiot!

You will need to work on memorizing Proverbs 18:21. This is a key verse. Write this verse out. __**Death and life are in the power of the tongue, And those who love it will eat its fruit.**__

What death words were spoken to you that you are still believing? __**Answers will vary**__

		Righteous man	Biblical Fool
Prov.	10:6	blessings	mouth conceals violence
	10:10		causes trouble, will be ruined
	10:11	fountain of life	conceals violence
	10:14	stores up knowledge	ruin is at hand,
	10:18		conceals hatred, has lying lips, spreads slander, is a fool
	10:19	restrains lips, wise	many words, transgression
	10:20	choice silver	worth little
	10:21	feeds many	lack of understanding, death
	10:31	flows with wisdom	perverted tongue will be cut out
	10:32	knows what is acceptable	is perverted

Questions to think about:

1. What sin of the tongue stands out most to you? **Answers will vary**

2. Why is this a sin? How does it go against who God is? **Answers will vary**

3. Is your self-talk defeating you or bringing you victory? **Answers will vary**

Week 4 / Day 2: Wise Words II

		Righteous Man	Biblical Fool
Prov.	11:9	be delivered	destroys neighbor
	11:13	trustworthy conceals a matter	talebearer reveals secrets
	12:6	will be delivered	lie in wait for blood
	12:13	will escape from trouble	snared by transgression of his lips
	12:14	satisfied with good	
	12:22	deal faithfully lying God's delight	lips an abomination to God
	12:25	makes glad those who are anxious	
	13:2	enjoys good	desires violence
	13:3	guards mouth – preserves his life	open wide his lips - ruin
	13:5	hates falsehood	acts disgustingly and shamefully
	14:3	lips will protect them	in mouth is rod for back
	14:5	trustworthy witness won't lie	false witness - lies
	14:23	labors for profit	mere talk leads to poverty
	14:25	trustful witness – saves lives	lies, is treacherous
	15:1	gentle answers turns away wrath	harsh word stirs up anger
	15:2	makes knowledge acceptable	spouts folly
	15:4	soothing tongue in tree of life	perversion crushes spirit
	15:7	spread knowledge	doesn't spread knowledge
	15:14	mind seeks knowledge	feeds on folly
	15:23	joy in an apt answer delight in timely word	
	15:26	pleasant words are pure	evil plan abomination to the Lord
	15:28	ponders how to answer	pours out evil things
	16:13	delight of kings is loved	
	16:21	sweet speech increases persuasiveness	
	16:23	heart instructs mouth adds persuasiveness to his lips	
	16:24	pleasant words are a honeycomb sweet to soul, healing to bones	
	16:28		perverse man spreads strife slanders separates intimate friend
	17:7		excellent speech not fitting for a fool or lying lips to a promise
	17:9		repeats matter

	separates intimate friends	
17:14	abandons quarrel	strife
17:20		perverted in language
		falls into evil
17:28		when silent is considered wise
		when closer lips is considered prudent

Questions to think about:

1. What sin of the tongue stands out most to you? **Answers will vary**

2. Why is this sin? How does it go against who God is? **Answers will vary**

3. The Lord by wisdom founded the __**earth**_____,
   By understanding He established the __**heavens**_____.
   By His knowledge the __**deeps**_____ were broken up
   And the skies drip with __**dew**_____.

Week 4 / Day 3: Wise Words III

		<u>Righteous Man</u>	<u>Biblical Fool</u>
Prov.	18:4	bubbling brook	
	18:6		brings strife, calls for blows
	18:7		mouth is his ruin
			lips are snare of soul
	18:8		words of whisperer are dainty morsels
			go deep into the body
	18:13		gives answer before he hears folly -
			and shame
	18:20	will be satisfied	
	18:21	life	death
	19:1		perverse in speech is a fool
	19:5		false witness, punishment tells lies
			will not escape
	19:9		not go unpunished, liars will perish
	19:22	kind	better to be poor than a liar
	19:28		makes mockery of justice
			spreads iniquity
	20:15	lips of knowledge	
		more precious than gold or jewels	
	20:17		obtains bread falsely

		mouth filled with gravel
20:19		slanderer reveals secrets
		gossip
20:20		curses mother and father
		lamp will go out in time of darkness
20:25		makes vow before inquiring
21:6		lying tongue, gets fleeting vapors
		pursuit of death
21:23	guards mouth and tongue	
	guards soul from troubles	
21:28	listens to truth	false witness will perish
	will speak forever	
22:10		contentious, scoffer, strife dishonor
22:11	speech is gracious	
	king will be friend	
22:14		mouth of an adultress a deep pit
		cursed of Lord will fall into it
23:15-16	speaks right	
	father will rejoice	
24:28-29		witness against neighbor without cause, deceitful
25:11	speaks words in right circumstances	
25:12	wise reprover	
25:13	faithful messenger	
	refreshes soul of masters	
25:14		boasts of gifts falsely
25:15	soft tongue breaks bones	
	(gets ruler to listen)	
25:18		bears false witness against neighbor
25:23-24		backbiting tongue, angry countenance
		contentious
26:2		curse without cause does –
		not alight
26:18-19		deceives neighbor and says, "I was
		only joking"
26:20	whisperer	contention
26:21		contentious, kindles strife
26:23		burning lips, wicked heart
26:24		disguises hat with lips but stores up –
		deceit in heart
26:25		speaks graciously but really 7
		abominations in heart,
26:28		lying tongue,
		hates those it crushes, flattering

		tongue works ruin
28:23	rebukes man, finds favor	flatters with tongue no favor
29:8	turn away anger	scorners start anger
29:20		hasty in words, no hope

Questions to think about:

1. What sin of the tongue stands out most to you? **Answers will vary**

2. Why is this sin? How does it go against who God is? **Answers will vary**

3. How does your mouth compare? **Answers will vary**

4. Are your words wounding others and yourself or giving grace to others and yourself? **Answers will vary**

5. The Lord by ___**wisdom**_____ founded the ___**earth**_____,
   By ____**understanding**_____ He established the __**heavens**_____.
   By His _**knowledge**_____ the __**depths**_____ were broken up
   And the skies ___**drip**_____ with ___**dew**___.

Week 4 / Day 4: The Tongue Can't Be Tamed

Who are you teaching? ___**Answers will vary**_____

James 3:2 continues, "For we all stumble in many ways. If anyone does not stumble in what he says, he is a _ **perfect**____ man, able to bridle the whole body as well." The Hebrew for *perfect* depicts a mature man making this not an impossible statement, but rather a goal to reach.

The tongue is compared to what three items in James 3:3-6?
1. **Bit in a horse's mouth**
2. **Rudder of a ship**
3. **Fire**

How much power over the rest of the body do these verses say the tongue has? __**a lot!**_____
James is actually setting you up for his admonishment found in verses 9-10. "From the same mouth come both _**blessings**_____ and __**curses**_____. My brethren, these things ought not to be this way."

"Does a fountain send out from the same opening both ___**fresh**_____ and ___**bitter**_____ water? Can a fig tree, my brethren, produce _**olives**_____, or a vine produce ___**figs**___? Nor can salt water produce fresh."

He asks, "Who among you is wise and understanding? Let him show by his good behavior his __**deeds**__ in the gentleness of wisdom."

Luke 6:45 says, "The good man out of the good treasure of his heart brings forth what is __**good**__; and the evil man out of the evil treasure brings forth what is __**evil**__; for his mouth speaks from that which fills his heart."

Looking at your words, what is the condition of your heart? __**Answers will vary**__

Finally, read James 3:17-18. List the characteristics of God's wisdom.

1. **Pure**
2. **Peaceable**
3. **Gentle**
4. **Reasonable**
5. **Full of mercy**
6. **Full of good fruits**
7. **Unwavering**
8. **Without hypocrisy**
9. **Righteous**

Are these characteristics of your mouth? __**Answers will vary**__

Proverbs 10:20: "The __**tongue**__ of the righteous is as choice silver, the __**lips**__ of the wicked is worth little."

Proverbs 10:31: "The __**mouth**__ of the righteous flows with wisdom, but the perverted __**tongue**__ will be cut out".

Proverbs 15:28: "The __**heart**__ of the righteous ponders how to answer, but the __**speech**__ of the wicked pours out evil things."

Proverbs 22:11: "He who loves purity of __**heart**__ and whose __**speech**__ is gracious the king is his friend."

Proverbs 23:15-16: "My son, if your __**heart**__ is wise, my own heart also will be glad; and my inmost being will rejoice when your __**lips**__ __**speak**__ what is right."

Proverbs 26:24: "He who hates disguises it with his __**lips**__, but he lays up deceit in his __**heart**__."

Proverbs 11:9: "With his __**mouth**__ the godless man destroys his neighbor, but through __**knowledge**__ the righteous will be delivered."

Proverbs 10:14: "Wise men store up __**knowledge**__, but with the __**mouth**__ of the foolish, ruin is at hand."

Questions to think about:

1. What does your tongue say about your heart? **Answers will vary**

2. What is the relationship between knowledge and the tongue? **Through knowledge the righteous will know how to answer.**

3. If you are having a hard time taming your tongue, what should your approach be to getting it under control? **Prayer, confession, repentance, accountability, filling up your mind with the word of God so your mind may be transformed.**

4. The **Lord** by **wisdom** founded the **earth** ,
   By **understanding** He **established** the **heavens** .
   By His **knowledge** the **depths** were **broken** **up**
   And the **skies** **drip** with **dew** .

Week 4 / Day 5: Last Word–Lying

Proverbs 12:19: "Truthful lips will be **established** forever, but a lying tongue is only for a **moment** ."

Proverbs 17:7: "Excellent speech is not fitting for a **fool** , much less are lying lips to a prince."

Proverbs 21:6: "The acquisition of treasures by a lying tongue is a **fleeting** **vapor** the pursuit of **death** ."

John 8:31-32 claims the, "Truth will set you **free** ."

1 John 2:16 tells you lies can also originate from Satan's domain–the world which you live in and your own mind. What is a lie the world is proclaiming? **You can do it all – career and family, you deserve the best, take care of number one, alcohol is fun and rewarding, you just need more stuff to be happy, it's all your parent's fault, etc…**

Anything you do apart from God is flesh. Look up John 5:15: "Apart from **Me** you can do nothing."

Ephesians. 6:12 reiterates this: "For our struggle is not against flesh and blood, but against the **rulers** , against the **powers** , against the **world** **forces** of this darkness, against the **spiritual** **forces** of wickedness in the heavenly places.

God doesn't leave you defenseless. What are your weapons listed in Ephesians 6:10-18?
1. **Truth**
2. **Righteousness**
3. **Preparation of the Gospel of Peace**
4. **Shield of Faith**
5. **Salvation**
6. **Sword of the Spirit**

7. **Prayer and Petition**

These weapons are powerful for the destruction of fortresses in spiritual realm and in the physical realm. But you must do what Ephesians 6: 11 commands you to do. What is this command? __**Put on the full armor of God**_____

Questions to think about:

1. Does lying come easily for you? **Answers will vary**

2. Is any lying justifiable? **No. Jesus is the truth. Anything less than the truth does not line up with His righteousness.**

3. What lies are you believing? **Answers will vary**

4. What is the truth about your justification (Rom. 3:24, 28, 5:1)? **It is accomplished as a gift by His grace through the redemption which is in Christ Jesus. We are justified by faith apart from the Law. We are at peace with God.**

5. What is the truth about your adoption (Rom. 8:15, 23, Eph. 1:5)? **We have received a spirit of adoption as sons (or daughters). We wait for the actualization of this adoption when our bodies are redeemed. Through the kindness of God's will we were predestined (pre-chosen) to be adopted.**

6. What is the truth about your reconciliation (Rom. 5:10, 2 Cor. 5:18, 20)? **It is accomplished through the death of Jesus, and we are saved by His life. He gave us the ministry of reconciliation as ambassadors for Christ.**

7. What is the truth about your sanctification (1 Cor. 1:2, 6:11)? **If you call on Jesus as your Lord you are sanctified through the washing clean of your sins by the blood of Jesus.**

Week 4 Group Discussion

The following questions were posed after the lessons this past week. Take time to discuss the answers and ask for responses. Additional verses are listed which will give you, the teacher, more insight. These lists are not exhaustive. Feel free to pray and ask God for other verses which answer these questions for you. You can study these ahead of time and then either ask the students look them up during class or just refer to them as you speak. Some of the questions might be personal. Don't push for answers. Either give an answer from your experience or move on.

1. What sins of the tongue stood out most to you? **Answers will vary**

2. How do these sins go against who God is? (! Peter 1:15-16) **God is holy, just, compassionate, full of grace and truth, merciful, thus words that proceed from our mouths which are not in line with these characteristics show sin in our hearts.**

3. How does your mouth compare to the righteous man's mouth? **Answers will vary**

4. Is your self-talk pleasing to God? **Answers will vary**

5. What is the relationship between your heart and your tongue? (Matt. 12:34) **The mouth speaks out of that which fills the heart.**

6. What is the relationship between knowledge and your tongue? (Prov. 2:6, 15:2, 15:4) **When we have knowledge, we can speak words of wisdom and soothing words of life.**

7. If you are having a hard time taming your tongue, what should your approach be to getting it under control? **Repentance, asking God to change your heart attitudes, asking the Holy Spirit to teach you as you open God's Word and do serious and consistent study. The Word will transform your mind and heart and the fruit of the Spirit (love, joy, peace, patience, kindness, goodness, faithfulness, gentleness, and self-control) will grow naturally as you plant yourself beside God's water of the Word (Jesus).**

8. Is any lying justifiable? (Ps. 25:5, 10, 26:3, John 8:3214:6, 1 John 1:6, 8, 2:4) **No. Telling the truth in love though takes discernment and discretion which comes from growing in God's word.**

9. What lies are you believing? **Answers will vary**

Week 5

Week 5 / Day 1: Destructive vs. Constructive Anger

James 1:19-20. You are to "Be quick to __**hear**__, slow to __**speak**__, and slow to __**anger**__, because the anger of man does not work the righteousness of God!"

Look at Ephesians 4:26. Anger is neither good nor bad. This verse says, "Be angry, but __**sin**__ not."

Proverbs 12:18 will help you to remember to control your angry responses. "There is one who speaks __**rashly**__ like the thrusts of a sword, but the tongue of the wise brings __**healing**__."

Questions to think about:

1. On a scale of 1-10, what is your anger level? **Answers will vary**

2. Do you tend to confront the people or events which make you angry, or do you tend to repress your anger and hurt? **Answers will vary**

3. Practice some pretend situations which would make you angry and role play aggressive behavior and assertive behavior. This could be done in your family as well. Take turns coming up with scenarios.

Week 5 / Day 2: Steps to Controlling Anger

Read 1 Peter 5:6-7: "Therefore humble yourselves under the __**mighty**__ hand of God, that He may exalt you at the proper time, casting all your anxiety on Him, because He __**cares**__ for you."

Matthew 11:28 carries a great promise. Write this promise here. __**Come to Me, all who are weary and heavy-laden, and I will give you rest.**__

Hebrews 12:15 says, "See to it that no one comes short of the grace of God: that no root of __**bitterness**__ springing up causes trouble, and by it many be defiled."

Read Ephesians 4:26-27, "Be angry, and yet do not sin; do not let the __**sun**__ __**go**__ __**down**__ on your anger, and do not give the devil an opportunity."

What's wrong with this picture? __**The train is going to derail because the tracks are not laid out straight.**__

Questions to think about:

1. How do you grieve the hurts of your life? **Answers will vary**

2. How full or empty is your emotional bucket? **Answers will vary**

3. What pulls your train–your emotions or God's Word? **Answers will vary**

4. My son, let them not vanish from your ___**sight**___ ;
   Keep sound wisdom and ___**discretion**___ ,
   So they will be life to your ___**soul**___
   And adornment to your ___**neck**___ .

Week 5 / Day 3: Choosing Forgiveness

Matthew 6:14-15: "For if you forgive others for their transgressions, your heavenly Father ___**will**___ also forgive you. But if you do not forgive others, then your Father ___**will**___ ___**not**___ forgive your transgressions."

That's something to think about. On a scale from 1 – 10, how important is it to God that you forgive others?
1   2   3   4   5   6   7   8   9   10
You should have circled 10

Questions to think about:

1. Is there anyone you need to forgive? Who? **Answers will vary**

2. What debt will you have to forgive in order to forgive this person? **Answers will vary, but may include: The right to an apology, money or other remuneration, what should have been yours (ie. A good childhood, a good marriage, etc…).**

3. How much did God forgive you? For what attitudes and actions has God forgiven you? **Answers will vary. He forgave my sin nature and all the putridness of the sins I committed from pride and selfishness to sins I acted out.**

4. What excuses do you give for not forgiving? **Answers will vary**

5. My son, let them not ___**vanish**___ from your ___**sight**___ ;
   Keep sound ___**wisdom**___ and ___**instruction**___ ,
   So they will be ___**life**___ to your ___**soul**___
   And ___**adornment**___ to your ___**neck**___ .

Week 5 / Day 4: Reasons Not to Forgive

Look at Philippians 3:13-14. "Brethren I do not regard myself as laying hold of it yet; but one thing I do: _ __**forgetting**__ what lies behind and reaching forward to what lies ahead, I press on toward the goal for the prize of the upward call of God in Christ Jesus."

Read 2 Corinthians 5:9-10.

What should your ambition be? ___**to be pleasing to God**___

Who will appear before the judgment seat? ___**each of us**___

What will be judged there? ___**each of us will be recompensed for our works (This is not salvation by works, but rather works that stemmed from our salvation).**___

Questions to think about:

1. Which of these excuses have you used? **Answers will vary**

2. What is your justifications for each excuse? **Answers will vary**

3. My son, ___**let**___ them not ___**vanish**___ from your ___**sight**___;
    Keep ___**sound**___ ___**wisdom**___ and ___**discretion**___,
    So they will be ___**life**___ to ___**your**___ ___**soul**___
    And ___**adornment**___ to ___**your**___ ___**neck**___.

Week 5 / Day 5: What Forgiveness Means

Questions to think about:

1. What inaccurate meanings of forgiveness did you hold as true? **Answers will vary**

2. Are you going to choose to forgive? **Answers will vary**

3. How are you enforcing healthy boundaries in a trying relationship? **Answers will vary**

Week 5 Group Discussion

The following questions were posed after the lessons this past week. Take time to discuss the answers and ask for responses. Additional verses are listed which will give you, the teacher, more insight. These lists are not exhaustive. Feel free to pray and ask God for other verses which answer these questions for you. You can study these ahead of time and then either ask the students look them up during class or just refer to them as you speak. Some of the questions might be personal. Don't push for answers. Either give an answer from your experience or move on.

1. What is your anger level? **1-10**

2. Do you tend to confront the people and events which make you angry or do you tend to repress your anger and hurt? **Answers will vary**

3. What are some constructive suggestions you think you could employ when you are angry? **Refer to chart in lesson Week 5 Day 1.**

4. Practice some pretend situations which would make you angry and role play aggressive behavior and assertive behavior. **Have fun with this. Ask different people to act out situations. Be careful not to make anyone uncomfortable though.**

5. How do you grieve the hurts of your life? **Answers will vary, but may include: wailing and weeping, talking to close friends or spouse, stuffing them, doing something physical, praying through them, or writing them out.**

6. How full or empty is your emotional bucket? **Answers will vary. We empty our buckets by talking out the hurts of the past with someone we trust.**

7. What should pull your train—your emotions or God's Word? (Col. 3:16, James 1:21) **God's Word.**

8. Which of the excuses in lesson four have you used? **Answers will vary**

9. What inaccurate meanings of forgiveness did you hold as true? **Answers will vary**

10. How are you enforcing healthy boundaries in a trying relationship? **Answers will vary, but may include: Limiting time spent with the person or on the phone with them, keeping them at an emotional distance, or seeing them only in a public place or with others present.**

Week 6

Week 6 / Day 1: Your Body and Food

Turn to 1 Corinthians 3:16. This verse will give you a foundation for this study. "Do you not know that you are a **temple** of **God**, and that the Spirit of God dwells in you?"

This picture is repeated in 1 Corinthians 6:19-20. "Or do you not know that your body is a **temple** of **the** **Holy** **Spirit** who is in you, whom you have from God, and that you are not your own? For you have been bought with a price; therefore, glorify God in your body."

According to 1 Corinthians 6:20, why should you glorify God with your body? **I have been bought with a price**

What was this price? **The blood of Jesus**

The blood of Jesus paid for your sins and you are now no longer to be a slave to sin, but to righteousness. And who is your righteousness? **Jesus**

List ways you can glorify God in your body. Include do's and don'ts.
Answers will vary, but may include:
Do: exercise, maintain a healthy weight, eat healthy foods, get a good night's sleep
Don'ts: smoke, remain overweight, drink alcohol, eat sugar

Proverbs 25:16 warns you about overeating. "Have you found honey? Eat only what you **need**, that you not have it in excess and vomit it."

1 Corinthians 6:12 According to this verse, what is lawful? **All things**
Are these things profitable? **Not all of them**

Proverbs 16:24 states, "Pleasant words are a honeycomb, Sweet to the soul and **healing** to the bones."

In Proverbs 25:27-28, what is a man who has no control over his spirit compared to? **Like a city that is broken into and without walls**

Proverbs 27:7 "A sated man (stomach is full and overflowing) loathes honey (that which is desirable and sweet and nutritious), but to a famished man any bitter thing is sweet."
Rewrite this Proverb in your own words: **Answers will vary**

Questions to think about:

1. The temple in Jerusalem was an exquisite structure. It was overlaid in gold. How important was this building to the Jewish worshipper? **They believe God dwelled there in the temple in the Holy of Holies. It was of the utmost importance.**

2. Is your body an exquisite dwelling place for the Lord? Why or why not. **Answers will vary**

3. What could you do to make your body a worthy dwelling place for the Holy Spirit? **Answers will vary**

Week 6 / Day 2: Drugs and Alcohol

Read Proverbs 23:20-21. What is their fate according to these verses? **poverty and rags**

Check out James 4:4 and 1 Corinthians 15:33. Summarize what these verses are teaching you. **It is important who your friends are. Bad friends will corrupt you.**

Proverbs 23:29-35 describes the life of an alcoholic pretty well.
What is wine compared to in verse 32? **the bite of a serpent and the sting of a viper**

What are the results of too much wine? There are 10 listed.
1. **Woe**
2. **Sorrow**
3. **Contentions**
4. **Complaining**
5. **Wounds without cause**
6. **Redness of eyes**
7. **Eyes will see strange things**
8. **Your mind will utter perverse things**
9. **As one who drowns**
10. **One who gets blown off of a mast**

Lastly, look at Proverbs 31:1-7. Who should never drink wine according to these verses? **Kings and rulers**

Who should drink wine? **Him who is perishing and those whose life is bitter**

James 4:7-8 says to "Submit therefore to God. **Resist** the devil and he will flee from you. **draw** near to God and He will draw near to you."

Read 1 Corinthians 10:13. "God is **faithful** who will not allow you to be tempted beyond what you are able, but with the temptation will provide a way of **escape** also, so that you will be able to endure it."

Questions to think about:

1. Are you in a position of authority? Do you wish to be in authority some day? **Answers will vary**

2. Those in authority shouldn't drink alcohol or do drugs. Why do you think this is? **They need clear minds to make important decisions. They need discernment to know who to befriend.**

3. Explain the quote, "What the parents do in moderation, the children will do in excess. **This can be the positive or the negative. Whatever your kids see you doing, they will embrace with passion.**

4. Give some positive and negative examples of this. **Positive: Serving others, giving, ministering, being compassionate, etc…**
   Negative: Yelling, anger, drugs, alcohol, sarcasm, judging, lying, criticizing, etc…

5. Then you will __**walk**__ in your way securely
   And your foot will not __**stumble**__.
   When you lie down, you will not __**be**__ __**afraid**__;
   When you lie down, your sleep will be __**sweet**__.

Week 6 / Day 3: Honoring Your Parents

Proverbs 20:20 says, "He who __**curses**__ his father or his mother, His lamp (eye) will go out in time of darkness."

In Exodus 20:12 God tells the Israelites to, "__**Honor**__ your father and your mother, that your days may be prolonged in the land which the Lord your God gives you."

From the text above, what two things can you do to honor your parents?
   1. **Don't speak badly about your parents**
   2. **Obey if you are under their roof, respect if you are an adult on your own.**

Proverbs 10:1 "A wise son makes a father __**glad**__, but a foolish son is a __**grief**__ to his mother."

Proverbs 13:1 "A wise son __**accepts**__ his father's discipline, but a scoffer does not listen to rebuke."

Proverbs 16:31 "A grey head is a crown of __**glory**__, It is found in the way of righteousness."

Proverbs 23:15-16 "My son, if your heart is __**wise**__, my own heart also will be __**glad**__; and my inmost being will rejoice when your lips speak what is right."

Proverbs 27:11 "Be wise, my son, and make my heart __**glad**__, that I may reply to him who reproaches me."

Proverbs 29:3 "A man who loves __**wisdom**__ makes his father glad, but he who keeps company with harlots wastes his wealth."

According to these verses, how can a son or daughter (even as an adult) make their parents glad? ____**By acting with wisdom, accepting discipline, not being a scoffer, speaking what is right, not keeping company with harlots (things contrary to God).**____

Questions to think about:

1. If your parents are alive, ask them if they feel like you honor them. Write their response here. **Answers will vary.**

2. If they have died, how can you honor them? **By not speaking bad about them. By being respectful about them.**

3. If you can't respect your parents because of their lifestyle choices, how can you still honor them? (You may not respect the president in the white house at any given time, but you can honor the position which he fills.) **Choose to not speak badly about them. Sometimes this means being vague, but not lying. It's okay to have a friend or two that you can share your hurts with about your parents, but limit it to those few.**

4. List some things that you are grateful for about your parents. **Answers will vary, but may include: for giving me life, for feeding me, for giving me shelter, for loving me, for disciplining me, for teaching me, for guiding me, etc...**

5. Then you will __**walk**__ in your way __**securely**__
   And your __**foot**__ will not __**stumble**__.
   When you __**lie**__ __**down**__, you will not __**be**__ __**afraid**__;
   When you __**lie**__ __**down**__, your sleep will be __**sweet**__.

Week 6 / Day 4: Your Heavenly Father

The steps of a man are established by the Lord,
And He __**delights**__ in his way.
When he falls, he will not be hurled headlong,
Because the __**Lord**__ is the One
who __**holds**__ __**his**__ __**hand**__.

Proverbs 30:17 gives you another admonition. "The eye that __**mocks**__ a father and __**scorns**__ a mother, the ravens of the valley will pick it out and the young eagles will eat it."

Proverbs 28:24 says: "He who __**robs**__ his father or his mother and says, 'It is not a transgression,' is the companion of a man who destroys."

Questions to think about:

1. How important is it to God that you honor you parents? **Extremely important because by honoring them we learn how to honor God.**

2. If someone does not honor their parents, they are worthy of death according to Romans 1:28-32. Why do you think that is? **This list which includes being disobedient to parents is a list of unrighteousness and comes from a depraved mind. When we are born again through the blood of Jesus, He transforms our minds and puts to death all sin including pride which is the root of all sin.**

3. How can you honor your parents? **Answers will vary. Even if there can be no relationship with them, you can pray for them. The next step for some might be sending cards, emailing, or calling. Others have a wonderful relationship with their parents of mutual respect and trust. Seek God in honoring your parents.**

4. List some characteristics of your Heavenly Father. **Compassionate, merciful, grace-giving, generous, loving, kind, disciplines for our good, unchanging, everlasting, patient, etc. If your list looks vastly different then you might need to seek out the characteristics of God from His Word. Psalms is a good place to start.**

5. Then you will __**walk**__ in __**your**__ __**way**__ __**securely**__
   And your __**foot**__ will __**not**__ __**stumble**__.
   When you __**lie**__ __**down**__, you will __**not**__ __**be**__ __**afraid**__;
   When you __**lie**__ __**down**__, your __**sleep**__ will be __**sweet**__.

Week 6 / Day 5: Raising Children

Read Deuteronomy 6:7. When should you teach your children about God? __**All the time!**__

Proverbs 29:15 says, "The rod and reproof give wisdom, but a child who gets his __**own**__ __**way**__ brings shame to his mother."

Questions to think about:

1. What are some of your children's natural bents? **Answers will vary**

2. What are their learning styles? **Answers will vary**

3. Do they have learning difficulties? How can you compensate for these? **Answers will vary**

Week 6 Group Discussion

The following questions were posed after the lessons this past week. Take time to discuss the answers and ask for responses. Additional verses are listed which will give you, the teacher, more insight. These lists are not exhaustive. Feel free to pray and ask God for other verses which answer these questions for you. You can study these ahead of time and then either ask the students look them up during class or just refer to them as you speak. Some of the questions might be personal. Don't push for answers. Either give an answer from your experience or move on.

1. The temple in Jerusalem was an exquisite structure. It was overlaid in gold. How important was this building to the Jewish worshipper? (1 Kings 8:10-1) **It was the center of the Jewish worship. They traveled to the temple at least once a year. The temple was where the Holy of Holies was located. God tabernacle there in their midst.**

2. Is your body an exquisite dwelling place for the Lord? What could you do to make your body a worthy dwelling place for the Holy Spirit? **Exercise, eat healthy, stop smoking, get more sleep, etc...**

3. Those in authority don't drink alcohol or do drugs. Why do you think this is? **They need to be clear headed to be able to make decisions, stay motivated, and to lead others.**

4. Explain the quote, "What the parents do in moderation, the children will do in excess." **To the negative and/or positive, your kids are watching you and will tend to do what you are doing taking it a step or more beyond what you do.**

5. Give some positive and negative examples of this. **Positive: Serving others, giving, church attendance, finding joy, healthy relationships, etc. Negative: alcohol, smoking, drugs, swearing, violence, etc.**

6. If you can't respect your parents because of their lifestyle choices, how can you still honor them? **Appreciate that they gave you life and fed, clothed, and housed you. Honor them because of their position as your parents. This does not mean you have to obey them if you are an adult. It does mean that you don't speak badly about them to others, you don't abuse them, and you make sure that they are taken care of in their older years.**

7. List some things you are grateful for about your parents. **Answers will vary**

8. Why is it important to God that you honor our parents? **They are God's representatives for you here on earth. By learning to honor them, you learn to honor God.**

9. List some characteristics of your Heavenly Father. (Ps. 103:8-14 and other Psalms) **Compassionate, patient, caring, giving, merciful, loving, jealous, grace-giving, forgiving, delights in you, unconditionally loves you, etc.**

Week 7

Week 7 / Day 1: Love and Marriage

Read Proverbs 12:4. "An excellent wife is the __**crown**__ of her husband, but she who __**shames**__ him is like rottenness in his bones.

Proverbs 18:22 says, "He who finds a wife finds a good thing and obtains __**favor**__ from the Lord.

Proverbs 19:14 claims, "House and wealth are an inheritance from fathers, but a __**prudent**__ wife is from the __**Lord**__."

What does it mean to be prudent? __**Wise in handling practical matters, careful about one's conduct.**__

In Proverbs 5:18 an attitude and the results are found. "Let your fountain be __**blessed**__, and __**rejoice**__ in the wife of your youth."

Proverbs 6:29: "So is the one who goes in to his neighbor's wife; Whoever touches her will not __**go unpunished**__.

Read Proverbs 5:2-14. What are the results of adultery? __**bitterness, will get cut, leads to death, give your vigor to others, give your years to the cruel one, strangers will be filled with your strength, hard-earned goods will go to an alien, groaning, flesh and body will be consumed, utter ruin**__

Questions to think about:

1. Are you a prudent wife? (If you are single, are you a prudent woman?) **Answers will vary.**

2. Why is it important to your marriage to keep growing closer to God? **As you and your husband both grow closer to God, you will grow closer to each other. If your husband is not growing closer to God, it is important that you continue to do so, so you can know God's answers, comfort, and direction.**

3. Why does Christian marriage matter to our culture and its view of God? **Christian marriage is an example to the world of God's relationship to each one of us. We will not draw the world to the cross if we are unhappy and divorcing for any reason.**

Week 7 / Day 2: Characteristics of Godly Men and Women

List the characteristics given for an older man.
 1. Temperate
 2. Dignified
 3. Sensible
 4. Sound in faith
 5. Sound in love
 6. Sound in perseverance

List the characteristics for an older woman.
 1. Reverent in their behavior
 2. Not malicious gossips
 3. Not enslaved to much wine
 4. Teaching what is good
 5. Encouraging the younger women

List the characteristics the older woman is to teach the younger women.
 1. To love their husbands
 2. To love their children
 3. To be sensible
 4. To be pure
 5. To be workers at home
 6. To be kind
 7. To be subject to their own husbands

What reason is given in Titus 2:5 for such behavior? __So that the word of God will not be dishonored.__

List the characteristics of a young man from Titus 2:6-8.
 1. Sensible
 2. An example of good deeds
 3. With purity in doctrine
 4. Dignified
 5. Sound in speech beyond reproach

Questions to think about:

 1. What might someone have to give up to be a worker at home? **A career, extra income, time away from children, self-importance, etc.**

 2. What might someone gain by being a worker at home? **Raising the children in the Word of God, consistency in discipline, security, relaxed atmosphere, obedience, joy of seeing children grow, memories, etc.**

3. If you are a young woman, what characteristics do you need to pray about for wisdom and practice? **Answers will vary**

4. If you are a seasoned woman of years, what characteristics do you need to pray about for wisdom and practice? **Answers will vary**

5. Do you know a godly man according to these lists? **Answers will vary**

6. Do not be afraid of **sudden** fear
   Nor of the onslaught of the **wicked** when it comes;
   For the Lord will be your **confidence**
   And will keep your **foot** from being caught.

Week 7 / Day 3: Characteristics of a Godly Man

Psalm 127:1 **Trusting in God to build his house (figuratively) and to keep watch**

Matthew 7:24 **Hearing God's word and acting upon it**

Ephesians 5:25, 28 **Loving his wife as Christ loves the church (sacrificially, unconditionally) as he loves his own body**

Ephesians 5:33 **Loving his own wife as himself**

1 Peter 3:7 **Living with his wife in an understanding way, as with someone weaker; showing her honor as a fellow heir of the grace of life**

Colossians 3:19 **Loving his wife and becoming embittered against her**

Ephesians 5:33 says, "Nevertheless, each individual among you also is to **love** his own wife even as himself, and the wife must see to it that she **respects** her husband."

Questions to think about:

1. If you are married, are you careful to support and encourage your husband? **Answers will vary**

2. Is criticism, complaining, or showing contempt an issue you need to purge from your life? **Answers will vary**

3. What are some words of respect and appreciation you can speak to your husband? **Answers will vary**

4. Singles, what characteristics should you be seeking in a male friend? **Sensible, an example of good**

deeds, with purity in doctrine, dignified, sound in speech beyond reproach

5. Do not be ___**afraid**___ of ___**sudden**___ fear
   Nor of the ___**onslaught**___ of the ___**wicked**___ when it comes;
   For the ___**Lord**___ will be your ___**confidence**___
   And will keep your ___**foot**___ from ___**being**___ ___**caught**___.

Week 7 / Day 4: Characteristics of a Godly Woman

Look at Proverbs 31:30. What characteristic is desired more than beauty? ___**The fear of the Lord**___

1 Timothy 2:9-10 What should come before beauty? ___**good works**___

1 Peter 3:4 What is precious in God's sight? ___**gentle and quiet spirit**___

Review the list of the seven characteristics an older woman is to teach a younger woman in Titus 2:4-5.
   1. **To love their husbands**
   2. **To love their children**
   3. **To be sensible**
   4. **To be pure**
   5. **To be workers at home**
   6. **To be kind**
   7. **To be subject to their own husbands**

Write Proverbs 10:1 here. ___**A wise son makes a father glad, But a foolish son is a grief to his mother.**___

What does Proverbs 11:13 say about talebearers? ___**They reveal secrets**___

Questions to think about:

1. Is it wrong to be beautiful and to enhance your looks with make up or pretty clothes? **Not as long as it is not your top priority. First we must have a gentle and quiet spirit. Drawing attention to your looks can be prideful. Let your motives be pure and glorifying to the Lord.**

2. What should be your first priority in preparing yourself for marriage? **Having a heart that fears the Lord and reverences His word. When you are content with just you and God, then you are ready to love another.**

3. How can you initiate changes into your communication patterns? **Be aware of your words. Take every thought captive to the obedience of Christ. Practice. Listen. Ask for feedback. Say you're sorry when you don't communicate well. Try again.**

4. Do not be ___**afraid**___ of ___**sudden**___ ___**fear**___
   Nor of the ___**onslaught**___ of the ___**wicked**___ when _**it**_ ___**comes**___ ;
   For the ___**Lord**___ will be ___**your**___ ___**confidence**___
   And will ___**keep**___ your ___**foot**___ from ___**being**___ ___**caught**___ .

Week 7 / Day 5: The Contentious Woman

Possible answers:

Proverbs 14:1: ___**Make sure my words and actions are building up my husband and children and not tearing them down. Make sure that I am industrious about keeping my home organized and meals made so that my days run smoothly.**___

Proverbs 14:4: This one will take some thought. Think about how people are more important than possessions. ___**Be careful about placing too much (to the extreme) importance on how the house looks, rather concern yourself with the people that live there.**___

Proverbs 18:22: ___**Being a good wife will bring blessings from God to my husband and thus to our home.**___

Proverbs 19:13: ___**Being contentious is annoying and burdensome to those in my home. I need to try to have a quiet and gentle spirit rather than a spirit of contention.**___

Proverbs 19:14: ___**You may or may not have possessions handed down from your fathers, but you can be a prudent wife and thus a gift to your husband from the Lord.**___

Proverbs 21:9: ___**Being contentious wears everyone around you down. They would be better off if you were not there. I need to be a blessing to my family.**___

Proverbs 21:19: ___**Being contentious is bitter and vexing to those around you. They would be better off in the desert. I need to work to have the joy of the Lord.**___

Proverbs 27:15-16: ___**It is impossible to restrain a contentious woman, and she annoys everyone around her. Instead of being contentious, I should try to work well with the others in my family. I should express hope and positive ideas rather than complaining and arguing.**___

Romans 12:18 says, "If possible, so far as it depends on you, be at peace with all men." What can you do to bring peace to your home? ___**Speak words of kindness and encouragement, do the housework to the expectations of my husband, react with humility, be quick to forgive, don't be quick to be offended, be filled with joy from my time with the lord, so that I can spread joy to others.**___

Questions to think about:

1. Are you a contentious woman? **Answers will vary**

2. If your answer to #1 is yes, what are you going to do to change that? **Answers will vary**

3. Is it okay to be contentious during your period or menopause? **No. We should walk by faith not by feelings.**

Week 7 Group Discussion

The following questions were posed after the lessons this past week. Take time to discuss the answers and ask for responses. Additional verses are listed which will give you, the teacher, more insight. These lists are not exhaustive. Feel free to pray and ask God for other verses which answer these questions for you. You can study these ahead of time and then either ask the students look them up during class or just refer to them as you speak. Some of the questions might be personal. Don't push for answers. Either give an answer from your experience or move on.

1. What does it mean to be prudent? **Acting with or showing care and thought for the future; wise in handling practical matters, careful about one's conduct. (You might ask to give some examples of prudent behavior in marriage.)**

2. Why is it important to your marriage to keep growing closer to God? **As you and your spouse grows closer to God, you will grow closer to each other. If your spouse is not growing closer to God, then you will need God even more to teach you and encourage you in your marriage.**

3. Why does Christian marriage matter to our culture and its view of God? **Marriage is the example that God chose to demonstrate His relationship to His people. The world is watching. When Christian marriages fail, it shows the world that Christianity "Doesn't work."**

4. Can someone work and make home a priority? **Yes, if there are small children in the home, a home based business is best. Working full-time and having a career will make it nearly impossible to make home a priority. Dad staying home while Mom works almost always leads to marital problems.**

5. What might someone gain by being a worker at home? **Raising the children in the Word of God, consistency in discipline, security, relaxed atmosphere, obedience, joy of seeing children grow, memories, etc.**

6. Are you a godly woman according to the lists? **Answers will vary**

7. Do you know a godly man according to these lists? **Answers will vary**

8. If you are married, how can you better support and encourage your husband? **Listen better, use my words to affirm and encourage him, serve him**

9 What are some words of respect and appreciation you can speak to your husband? **Answers will vary, but may include: "Good job!" "I'm so glad I married you." "Thank you for helping me. I'm glad you are so strong." "You sure a a good provider for our family."**

9. Is it wrong to be beautiful and to enhance your looks with make up or pretty clothes? **Not if your motive is to look your best to give God the glory. Your priority needs to be to fear the Lord and to live a pure and holy life.**

10. How can you initiate changes into your communication patterns? **Be aware of your words. Take every thought captive to the obedience of Christ. Practice. Listen. Ask for feedback. Say you're sorry when you don't communicate well. Try again.**

11. What are the characteristics of a contentious woman? **Boisterous, complaining, critical, argumentative, never pleased, not content, looking for a fight, always right, never speaks words of respect to her husband, and is not filled with the Spirit of God.**

Week 8

Week 8 / Day 1: Wise Woman of Proverbs 31

Look at verse 10. What is an excellent wife compared to? _____**fine jewels**_____

Notice she is not just as good as fine jewels, but her worth is far above jewels! What else in your study of Proverbs was compared to jewels? __**Wisdom**_____ (Prov. 3:13-15).

In verse 12, the excellent wife has what kind of actions for her husband? __**good**_____

What area of homemaking is challenging for you? __**Answers will vary**_____ . What can you do to improve? _____**Answers will vary**_____

Questions to think about:

1. What is your favorite jewel? Do you own one? **Answers will vary**

2. How can you garner trust from your husband? (Singles: do your friends consider you trust worthy? What can you do to show that trust?) **By being trustworthy in words and actions, keeping secrets between the two of you including your intimate life, doing what you say you will do.**

3. What chores of goodness can you begin to do for your husband? (Singles: for a friend?) **Answers will vary (My husband feels loved when I set out his underclothes for him while he is in the shower.)**

4. What attitude do you need to acquire to serve your husband better? (Singles: to serve others better?) **Humility, service, quiet joy, fun spirit**

Week 8 / Day 2: Woman's Work and Wealth

Read verse 16. "She considers a field and __**buys**__ it; from her __**earnings**_____ she plants a vineyard."

What can you do to earn extra income while making your home your priority? __**Answers will vary**_____

Verse 17 says, "She girds herself with __**strength**__ and makes her arms strong."

What do you do for exercise? __**Answers will vary**

What spiritual exercise are you doing daily to strengthen your faith? __**Reading the Bible, praying, praising, studying God's word with others, memorizing Scripture, listening to sermons, tuning in to Christian radio**_____

"She senses that her gain is __**good**_____; her lamp does not go out at night."

Questions to think about:

1. How much sleep do you need? **Answers will vary, but 8 hours is recommended.**

2. What needs to be organized at your house? **Answers will vary**

3. What homemaking skill can you learn and employ for the good of others? **Answers will vary**

Week 8 / Day 3: A Wise Woman's Sphere of Influence

List the people the Proverbs 31 woman influences for good.
1. **Her husband**
2. **Her children**
3. **Her household staff**
4. **The poor and needy**

What does Colossians 3:12-13 say you should put on?
1. **Heart of compassion**
2. **Kindness**
3. **Humility**
4. **Gentleness**
5. **Patience**
6. **Forbearance**
7. **Forgiveness**

Add to them the garments of Proverbs 31:25. "__**Strength**_____ and ____**dignity**_____ are her clothing, and she smiles at the future."

In verse 26 what two things also come from this same source? ___**wisdom and the teaching of kindness**_____

Questions to think about:

1. What household chore seems hard for you to accomplish? **Answers will vary**

2. What's your plan to get better at this task? **Answers will vary**

3. What steps can you take to becoming a woman of positive influence? **Answers will vary**

Week 8 / Day 4: The Fear of the Lord

Read verse 27-31. Underlying all of Proverbs 31 woman's activities is what motivation? ___**the fear of the Lord**_____

You learned in Proverbs 1:7, "The fear of the Lord is the beginning of ___**knowledge**_____." In Psalms 111:10, you find, "The fear of the Lord is the beginning of ___**wisdom**_____."

You will have no fear of ___**condemnation**_____ from God (Romans 8:1).

What praises do you receive from the work of your hands? ____ **Answers will vary** ____

Questions to think about:

1. Have you called your mother blessed? Now would be a good time! **Answers will vary**

2. Have your children called you blessed? **Answers will vary**

3. Does your husband praise you? What does he praise you for? **Answers will vary**

Week 8 / Day 5: Your Story Through the Names of God

How would you fill out the rest of this statement?
God is... ___ **Answers will vary** _____

Questions to think about:

1. Choose a couple of God's names and share how He has shown Himself faithful in these areas in your life. **Answers will vary**

Week 8 Group Discussion

The following questions were posed after the lessons this past week. Take time to discuss the answers and ask for responses. Additional verses are listed which will give you, the teacher, more insight. These lists are not exhaustive. Feel free to pray and ask God for other verses which answer these questions for you. You can study these ahead of time and then either ask the students look them up during class or just refer to them as you speak. Some of the questions might be personal. Don't push for answers. Either give an answer from your experience or move on.

1 What is your favorite jewel? Do you own one? How is a good wife like a jewel? **Answers will vary. A good wife is like a jewel because her kind and sweet spirit shines and makes her husband look good. She is desired and valuable to her husband.**

2. How can you garner trust from your husband? (Singles: do your friends consider you trust worthy? What can you do to show that trust?) **By being trust worthy in words and actions, keeping secrets between the two of you including your intimate life, doing what you say you will do.**

3. What attitude do you need to acquire to serve your husband better? (Singles: to serve others better?) **Humility, serve, joy, fun spirit, submission (not being a doormat, but being able to freely share your opinion, but leaving the final decision to your husband and graciously getting behind his decisions.)**

4. What needs to be organized at your house? **Answers will vary**

5. What steps can you take to becoming a woman of positive influence? **Grow in holiness through Bible study and prayer, put yourself in leadership, put yourself in situations where you regularly interact with others.**

6. Does your husband praise you? What does he praise you for? **Answers will vary**

Choose a couple of God's names and share how He has shown Himself faithful in these areas in your life. **Answers will vary.**

Endnotes

[1] Jaime Dean, "Giving Account", *World Magazine*, (Retrieved from https://world.wng.org/2009/07/giving_account).

[2] Lord, Peter, *Hearing God,* (Grand Rapids: Baker Book House, 1988), 9.

[3] Ibid, 30.

[4] J. D. Davis, *Davis Dictionary of the Bible*, (Nashville: Broadman Press, 4th revision), 477.

[5] Mvelopes, (https://www.mvelopes.com).

[6] Elizabeth Achelis, *Journal of Calendar Reform*, 1954, (myweb.ecu.edu/mccartyr/Russia.html).

[7] "RG LeTourneau – Earthmoving Innovator", *Giants for God,* (Retrieved from www.giantsforgod.com/rg-letourneau/).

[8] Victor Cohn, "The 'Miracle' of the Mayo Clinic", *The Washington Post,* Jan. 6, 1987, (Retrieved from https://www.washingtonpost.com/archive/lifestyle/wellness/1987/01/06/the-miracle-of-the-mayo-clinic/5bcee1f2-57d0-4cbb-9436-bf2ebf88e10b/?utm_term=.9a93ed5c1c00).

[9] Dara Halydier, "What Really Happened at the Cross", (Retrieved from http://www.abidingtruthministry.com/?page_id=3146).

[10] J. Vernon McGee, *Thru the Bible*, vol. 5, 1 Corinthians – Revelation, (Nashville: Thomas Nelson, 1983), 279.

[11] Dr. Chris Thurman, *The Lies We Believe*, (Nashville: Thomas Nelson, 1999).

[12]Nancy L. DeMoss, *The Lies Women Believe: And the Truth That Sets Them Free,* (Chicago: Moody Press, 2001).

[13]Beth Moore, *Praying God's Word: Breaking Free from Spiritual Strongholds,* (Nashville: B&H Publishing Group, 2009).

[14]Dr. Robert McGee, *Search for Significance: Seeing Your True Worth Through God's Eyes,* 2 ed. (Nashville: Thomas Nelson, 2003).

[15]Anabel Gillian, *The Confident Woman: Knowing Who You Are in Christ,* (Eugene, OR: Harvest House, 1993).

[16]Les Carter and Frank Minerth, *The Anger Workbook: A 13-Step Interactive Plan to Help You.,* (Nashville: Thomas Nelson, 1993), 23.

[17]Ibid, 3.

[18]Ibid, 4.

[19]"Dictionary.com", (Retrieved from http://www.dictionary.com/browse/bitterness?s=t).

[20]Les Carter and Frank Minerth, *Choosing to Forgive: 12 Steps to Forgiveness,* (Nashville: Thomas Nelson, 1997).

[21]Les Carter and Frank Minerth, *The Forgiveness Workbook: A 12 Part Comprehensive Plan to Overcome Your Struggle to Forgive and to Find Lasting Healing,* (Nashville: Thomas Nelson, 1997).

[22]Carter and Minerth, *Choosing to Forgive, 23.*

[23]Carter and Minerth, *The Forgiveness Workbook,* 16.

[24]Ibid

[25]Henry Cloud and John Townsend, *Boundaries: When to Say Yes When to Say No — To Take Control of Your Life,* (Grand Rapids: Zondervan, 1992).

[26]Anne Katherine, *Boundaries: Where You End and I Begin,* (Center City, MN: Hazelden, 1991).

[27]Unknown author, "Letting go", Inspiration Peak, (Retrieved from http://www.inspirationpeak.com/cgi-bin/poetry.cgi?record=77

[28]Bill Gothard, quoted by Susan Pippin, *Susan's Coffeebreak: 365 Daily Devotions,* (Maitland, FL: Xulon Press, 2011), 97.

[29]Robert McGee, *Search for Significance,* (Nashville: W Publishing Group, 2003).

[30]Robert McGee, Jim Craddock, and Pat S. McGee, *The Parent Factor*, (Nashville: Rapha Publishing, 1989).

[31]Cynthia Tobias, *The Way They Learn*, (Colorado Springs: Focus on the Family. 1998).

[32]Carol Barnier, *The Big What Now Book of Learning Styles* (United Kingdom: Emerald Books; 2009).

[33]Jeffrey Freed and Laurie Parsons, *Right Brained Kids in a Left Brained World*, (New York: Simon & Schuster, 1988).

[34]Gary Chapman, *The Five Love Languages of Children*, 3 ed. (Chicago: Northfield Publishing, 2012).

[35]Dara Halydier, *As They Sit and Stand: A Resource and Guide for Teaching Your Children the Bible*, (Early, TX: Dara Halydier, 2014). Available at http://www.abidingtruthministry.com/?product=2386 or on Amazon.

[36]*Brainy Quotes*, "Rita Rudner Quotes", (Retrieved from https://www.brainyquote.com/quotes/authors/r/rita_rudner.html).

[37]*Brainy Quotes*, "Martin Luther Quotes", (Retrieved from https://www.brainyquote.com/quotes/quotes/m/martinluth138958.html).

[38]Perry Tankley, "Marriage Takes Three", (Retrieved from http://www.kimberlyapril.com/marriage-takes-three/).

[39]Anabel Gillham, *The Confident Woman*, (Harvest House Publishers: Oregon), 153-154.

[40]Ibid

[41]Dara Halydier, *Living Beautifully: Practical Proverbs for Women Book 1*, (Brownwood, TX: Dara Halydier, 2017).

[42]Willard F. Harley, Jr. *His Needs, Her Needs: Building an Affair-Proof Marriage*, (Grand Rapids: Fleming H. Revell, 2001).

[43]Cooper, Darian B, *You Can Be the Wife of a Happy Husband: Discovering the Keys to Marital Success,* (St. Louis: Destiny Image Publishing, 2011).

[44]John McArthur, Grace to You, "The Proverbs 31 Woman", (Retrieved from https://www.gty.org/library/sermons-library/80-168/the-proverbs-31-woman).

[45]Dr. Claude Mariottini, *Dr. Claude Mariottini – Professor of Old Testament*, "Who was King Lemuel?" posted May 18, 2009, (Retrieved from https://claudemariottini.com/2009/05/18/who-was-king-lemuel/).

[46]William Ross Wallace, "What Rules the World", (1865).

[47]Ken Hemphill, *Names of God,* (Nashville: B&H Books, 2001).

About the Author

Dara Halydier lives in Texas with her husband of 33 years. They have had many adventures together raising and homeschooling five boys, and they look forward to more escapades with their seven grandchildren. Dara has been a pastor's wife, mentor, leader of homeschool groups, piano teacher, and friend. She has learned spiritual lessons the hard way—experience! She battles chronic pain with spina bifida and numerous back surgeries, survived and thrives after a childhood of abuse, and loves to sing the praises of her Father God.

www.ingramcontent.com/pod-product-compliance
Lightning Source LLC
Chambersburg PA
CBHW081228090426
42738CB00016B/3220